PERSONAL PLEASURES

❧ *Personal Pleasures* ❧

Rose Macaulay

A COMMON READER EDITION
THE AKADINE PRESS

Personal Pleasures

A COMMON READER EDITION published 1998
by The Akadine Press, Inc., by arrangement with
The Estate of Rose Macaulay.

A COMMON READER EDITION and fountain colophon are trademarks
of The Akadine Press, Inc.

ISBN 1-888173-35-1

10 9 8 7 6 5 4 3 2 1

Pleasure . . . .
That reeling goddess with the zoneless waist
And wand'ring eyes

W. COWPER. *The Task*

But every pleasure hath a payne, they say.

GEORGE CHAPMAN
The Blind Beggar of Alexandria

FRATRIBUS SORORIBUSQUE

FOREWORD

COMPILING, as I recently did, a selection from the records of the pleasures enjoyed by other people has forced on me the conclusion that other people, though they have doubtless (between them) enjoyed all the pleasures accessible to our mortal state, have left very many of them unrecorded in print. Be that as it may, everyone has his own pleasures, enjoyed after his own manner, and much perusal of those of others has moved me to record a few of my own. Necessarily only a few. Had I but world enough and time, I might have continued this agreeable pastime for ever, leaving no joy unspelt, unwrit, no mirthful hour unsung. When I look through my collection and note its gaps, I feel, like Clive, amazed at my own moderation. There are here, for instance, no games; that is, no set games, with rules. There are all too few picnics, no riding, no separate heading for conversation, no presents, no money, no friends, no maps. There are a thousand pleasures, even of my own, left unrecorded in this brief choice. But a choice it had to be, owing, as I say, to this perhaps fortunate limitation of world and time which sets so brief a term to all our undertakings. So I have set down a few pleasures randomly, as they came to mind. They are pleasures of different, sometimes of contrary, moods; they include parties, and not going to parties, believing and disbelieving, solitude and showing off, and other seemingly opposed diversions.

But how true it is that every pleasure has also its reverse side, in brief, its pain. Or, if not wholly true, how nearly so. Therefore I have added to most of my pleasures the little flavour of bitterness, the flaw in their perfection, the canker in the damask, the worm at the root, the fear of loss, or of satiety, the fearful risks involved in their very existence, which tang their sweetness, and mind us of their mortality and of our own, and that nothing in this world is perfect.

CONTENTS

ABROAD

ABROAD

THE great and recurrent question about Abroad is, is it worth the trouble of getting there? Delicious as is the prospect we see beyond this travail, shall we be enabled to conquer sloth's enticements, and emerge from what Mr. Thomas Coryat, that enterprising Jacobean tourist, contemptuously termed our domestical lurking corners? Is there any peace, the voice of indolence protests, in ever climbing up the climbing wave?

Let us hearken rather to the stirring exhortations of Mr. Coryat, who must have been minded much like Mr. Thomas Cook, and spoke with his very accents. "Let us," cried Mr. Coryat, "propose before our eyes that most beautiful theatre of the universe, let us behold whatever is abroad in the world, let us look into provinces, see cities, run over kingdoms and empires. Surely we shall find," said he, hopefully, "those people which have used no journeys to be rude, slothful, uncivil, rough, outrageous, foolish, barbarous, void of all humanity, civility and courteous entertainment, proud, arrogant, puffed up with self love and admiration of themselves, also effeminate, wanton, given to sleep, banquetings, dice and idleness, corrupted with the allurements of all pleasures and the enticements of all concupiscence."

3

But this is getting to sound agreeable; if home offers all that, one might do worse than stay there. Our tourist perceives this, and hurries on in different vein: "Such is the sweetness of travelling and seeing the world, such the pleasure, such the delight, that I think that man void of all sense and of a stony hardness, which cannot be moved with so great a pleasure. . . . O sluggish, abject, servile, and most dejected mind, which includeth itself within the narrow bounds of his own house."

Perhaps it is the expense you dread? "As though the dice and dicing box, domestical idleness, domestical luxury, and the gulf of domestical gourmandizing, doth not far exceed the necessary charges of travel."

That is as may be. Perhaps one would do well not to balance the nicely calculated less and more, but to remember the spring cleaning, or the house painting, and consider how many by their travels have procured themselves evasion from domestical calamities and miseries.

Arise, then, from abject and home-keeping sloth. Cease to regard with effeminate distaste those hurdles which stand between you and Abroad, looming high, barred, enthorned, only by the strong to be o'er-leapt. Do tickets, passports, money, travellers' cheques, packing, reservations, boat trains, inns, crouch and snarl before you like those surly dragons that guard enchanted lands? A little firmness, a nice mingling of industry, negligence and guile, and the hurdles will be leaped, the dragons passed; snapping your fingers at what you have left undone, you launch yourself into space.

Yes, you are on the boat train; you make once more the Grand Tour; you are full steam ahead for Dover, for Boulogne, for the silver seas whereon trumpet and pipe these enticing sirens against whose penetrating call even Ulysses would have cered his ears in vain. Hola, Captain! where is the packet for France? Here, Sir, here, and a fair wind in our sails. Honest gentlemen who will for Calais, let them make haste. To Calais ho! Aboard ho! The wind is at North, North, and North-West. Is the ship well armed, Captain? Fear nothing, Sir, for the ship is very well equipped with artillery and munition. Go into the prow. The wind blows, the tide swells, see the waves mount. The sea begins to rise and rage from the very bottom. See how those huge waves beat against the sides of our ship. Hear you these terrible whirlwinds, how they sing over our sailyards? We shall have by and by a storm. The tempest makes a great noise. The heaven begins to thunder from above. It thunders, it lightens, it rains, it hails; it is best to strike sail, and to veer the cables. This wave will carry us to all the Devils. . . . O my friends on shore! O thrice and four times happy are those who are on firm land setting of beans! O St. James, St. Peter, and St. Christopher! O St. Michael, St. Nicholas! O God we are now at the bottom of the sea. I give eighteen hundred thousand crowns to him who will set me a land. Let's land, let's go a shore. Captain, I will give you all that I have in the world to set me a shore. Will you go a shore in the midst of the ocean sea, Sir? What a horrible tempest! By St. Grison what means this? Shall we take our sepulture here among these waves? I pardon all the world. I die, my friends. Fare you all well.

The tempest is now ended. Oh, it is fine weather again. A fig for the waves. We are in the haven of Calais. We are saved. Cannoneer, shoot off a piece of artillery. Les passeports, s'il vous plait. Oh, yes, indeed, anything. Par ici pour la douane. By all means yes, even that. How delighted I am to be arrived! Here is all my luggage, and all its keys.

Yes, you may look at everything, tumble everything about. No, nothing to declare, nothing at all; still, by all means rummage. This one too? Of course. And now you will chalk them; that is nice. Now for the train; allons, allons, facteur! Second-class, n'est-ce-pas. No, nothing else about it matters, and I have no reserved seat. Put me anywhere. What? All reserved? Then I must wait for another train, n'est-ce-pas. No, I never reserve seats in advance, it is quite too much trouble. What I say is, why make a business of what is meant for a pleasure? If a railway ticket does not get me on to a French train, then France is not the land of liberty, equality, or fraternity. But then, one never supposed that it was. There will be another train presently, free to all? That is excellent news. I will settle down; I will wait. Attention, there is a train. Allons, allons, facteur; deuxième classe, s'il vous plait. Ah, Ah, I am on the train, n'est-ce-pas. Mettez mes bagages on the rack, on the seat, on the floor, all about me. Je suis bien entourée, n'est-ce-pas. But see, there lacks one bagage; where can it be? Oh, Oh, you have left it on the platform over there. Vite, vite, facteur! The train departs. You have not been vite enough; the train is departed. I shall not see my bag again. Je me plaindrai au consul anglais.

Eh bien. Life is like that. Abroad, in particular, is like that. And now I am abroad; I am entrained; I am launched on my enchanting error across Europe. Where shall I go? France, Spain, Italy, everywhere; perhaps even Portugal. How fast and how loud foreigners talk! It is a gift; the British cannot talk so loud or so fast. They have too many centuries of fog in their throats. Besides, they are nervous; they dare not talk loud; they mumble and murmur, afraid lest some one will hear. Never mind them; forget them; too many of them are, indeed, on this train, on all trains, since the English cannot keep still or stay at home, but still we will ignore and forget them, we will feign that we are alone abroad among the foreigners. Allons, allons, mes braves compagnons! To Paris ho! But only to make a change of train; we will not linger in Paris, it is drab and cold. Across it quickly to the Gare de Lyons, the Gare d'Orléans, and off to the South. East or west, Marseilles or Bordeaux, Mediterranean or Atlantic, Italy or Spain, it matters not, it is all south. Palms, pines, pepper, eucalyptus, oranges, lemons, juniper, myrtle; Alps, Apennines, Pyrenees; Basque, Catalan, Castilian, Mallorquin, Ligurian, Tuscan, Sicilian,

Venetian, Greek, Portuguese—any language you like,
I have the phrase-books of some of them, and can do
the rest by signs. To Greece with little English ladies
and schoolmasters, questing after ancient Hellenes.
Ἀθήναζε!ʼΟλυμπίαζε! To Athens! To Olympia! Ἀθηναι
εἰσι καλαί, Athens are beautiful. Oh, how beautiful
Athens are! That is to say, they are vulgar and modern
and dirty, but never mind, we rummage among them,
we find the Acropolis. Schoolmasters, dons, little eager
ladies, we swarm about the Acropolis, among the modern Hellenes, who do not comprehend their own
ancient tongue when we speak it to them, who desire
only that we should give them money. Over the hills
to Corinth; Greece is terra-cotta coloured, and silver
with olives; tortoises and lizards scuttle over it. The
Vale of Tempe is dark and deep, and Peneius shines in
it like an agate. All the plains of Thessaly; Olympus,
Ossa and Pelion; Thermopylæ, Parnassus, Thebes,
Cithæron; the schoolmasters, the dons, the little ladies,
are overwhelmed. Greece is really excessive. One cannot idle in it, or be stupid or inert, no, not for a
moment, or one will miss something, one wastes one's
time, since it is possible that one will not be this way
again. One cannot, in Greece, be happy merely in
being Abroad. For Abroad, Italy and France and Spain
and Czecho-Slovakia and Scandinavia and the Amer-
icas and the South Seas are better. Back, then, to Italy;
Sicily and Calabria and Naples; look how Vesuvius
smokes! Stroll about Pompeii, so gay, so coloured, so
still; if you are encouraging, one of the custodians

will show you a house freshly dug, and perhaps embrace you in it. Rome, Florence, Siena, Umbria, Venice, the lakes; having seen all these, settle down on the Ligurian sea shore and bathe. Nothing to see here but sea and shore and fishermen and nets and mountains and some small town. No buildings, no pictures, no churches, nothing but Abroad. Buon giorno, signorina, sta bene oggi? Benissimo, grazie, signore; mi bagnerò nel mare, dopo di prendere il caffé. Caffè latte! how it froths into the thick white cup! Sugar tablets wrapped in paper, coarse white crusty roll, church bells clanging, fishermen shouting, small waves lisping on the sand. You can stay in the sea all day if you wish, coming out to dry and toast, and slipping in again. It is deep sky-blue, and there is a rock far out on which you can sit. Great Britain can give you buildings, picture galleries, cities, (though of no great moment and of inconsiderable antiquity) and scenery, but only Abroad can give you real bathing.

For that matter, only Abroad can provide a great deal else. Meals, for example, in the streets. Trams that blow horns; indeed, traffic horns in general play a sweeter, liltier music than ever they play in Britain. How their gay tune, on two notes, like a cuckoo's song reversed, lifts the heart! Mountains of a height, a jaggedness, a grandeur, that surpasses those of Caledonia, Westmorland and Wales. Terraces climbing up their lower slopes, set with olives, chestnuts, figs, and vines. Large white oxen drawing loads of marble. Mules drawing sand. Nets being hauled in from the sea heavy with bianchetti, and perhaps a tunny or two. Processions round the town, led by nasally chanting acolytes and magnificently dressed wax saints, and followed by the citizens. Rose petals scattered and flung from every window on to the Corpus Christi procession: Little St. John, the Baptist, his hair just released from a week's curling-papers, leading his unruly lamb in the procession on his day. Brown and beautiful Basques dancing the fandango in the squares after a pelota match on Sunday evening. Redwood forests, giant cactuses in a pale Arizona desert, palms and orange trees and futbal in the plaza, the great blue sweep of Mexican mountains, the brown adobe of Mexican villages, the yucca standing high like blossoming swords, the wild roads not mended since the last revolution, the tiny burros carrying Mexicans, the estancias, haciendas, chile con carne, tortillas, the comida con vino incluso, the mandolins twanging in the plaza while you sit on the pavement and eat. The hot dog stalls, the camping cabins, San Francisco on her hills above the Golden Gate, Santa Barbara in white adobe, set with lit fir-trees on a warm Christmas night, San Diego, Tia Juana, and the Old Spanish Trail. The Florida seas and their leaning palmettos, the Keys and their twisted mangroves, Cuba across the straits. A small Provençal estaminet on the foothills, a mountain road twisting above it. Sunshine and warmth, sunshine and warmth, and the scent of lemons on the air. And, naturally, foreigners. I do not prefer foreigners to the English, except that they speak another language.

Otherwise they are, I find, essentially much the same, though the Italians and Spanish are handsomer and browner, and the Americans more cordial. But they all belong to Abroad, that great, that delightful English picnic. So, like Walt Whitman, I make a salute to all foreigners. As he so exuberantly exclaimed, "You Sardinian, you Bavarian, Swabian, Saxon, Wallachian, Bulgarian! You Roman, Neapolitan, you Greek! You little Matador in the arena at Seville! You mountaineer living lawlessly on the Taurus or Caucasus! You thoughtful Armenian! You Japanese! All you continentals of Asia, Africa, Europe, Australia, indifferent of place! You benighted roamer of Amazonia! You Patagonian, you Feejeeman! . . . I do not say one word against you! Salut au monde!"

He was right. It is all Abroad, all that vast camping-ground, pleasure garden or paradise in which we may wander at large; or might until recently, when passports, bureaucracy and suspicion are attempting to hamper and limit our tranquil and happy errors over our errant celestial ball. Les passeports s'il vous plait! Par ici pour la douane! Apra la sua valigia! Sin duda quejaré al consul ingles. I guess we'll have to put you on Ellis Island, if that's all the dollars you have.

Yes; we are hampered, invigilated, kept in on every side, very likely flung into gaol, directly we step into our pleasure-ground. But, when governments and their watch-dogs have done their worst, it is still Abroad.

ALBUM

ALBUM

How enchanting your relations are! Mine, too, look much the same. I suppose people do; I mean, so much depends on the clothes, does it not? I like your aunts; how they ripple from the waist down, bending in the middle like swans; their hair piled high in chignons; see, how much of it they have—or was some, perhaps, attached, or rolled over cushions? Your Aunt Amy, did you say? What long ear-rings! She is very elegant, *mondaine*, refined, yet *capable*, do you not think, *de tout*? Or was she not? Married a curate, do you say? One wonders what life in the curate-house was like, after your Aunt Amy entered it. Nine children? So that was what it was like. Yes, I see, here they all are. The little boys in sailor suits or jerseys, holding bats; the little girls in sashes, their hair cut across their foreheads. Du Maurier children. Oh, yes, I see, that is Phyllis, and there are Olive and Ruth. I should know them anywhere; by the way, I hear Ruth's grandchildren are at that fashionable school in Dorset, and can already change wheels, top batteries, and milk cows. They are going to learn to read next year, you say? At ten and twelve? Isn't that a little soon? One is so afraid of over-exciting their brains. Still, if they *want* to learn, anything is better than repressing them. . . .

A clergyman: of course, Aunt Amy's husband. A Tractarian, was he? Well, he was a little late for that; but I see what you mean, he was whatever High Church clergymen were in the eighties. Wrote tracts about the Eastward Position? I think he was so right. And, of course, they all face that way now, so that shows.

Who is that old military man? He looks like a splendid walrus, with his long whiskers. Your paternal grandfather? Of course; the General. Didn't he fight in the Crimea? Charged with the Light Brigade? How exciting! And how fortunate that he was one of those who rode back. He looks the kind of military man who might have been very much annoyed with whoever it was who had blundered. I should not care to face your grandfather if I had blundered. The lady in the crinoline is your grandmother, of course. She looks full of spirit; I dare say she needed it all. A crinoline gives such dignity, such deportment. No one could look *dowdy* in a crinoline. How her chatelaine hangs over it, full of the store-room keys. What a bore, to have to unlock the store-room whenever anyone wanted stores. I suppose stores are used by the cook daily, and always at the most inconvenient moment.

Look at those lovely girls, all in crinolines, ready to swim along like balloons in a breeze. Your great aunts? They are very sweet. No doubt they had a delightful time, waltzing, shooting with bows and arrows, riding, skating with gentlemen (for there was real ice in those days, was there not?) See, there is one of them on a horse, in a long habit, her hair in a net under a dear little feathered hat. Great-aunt Helen? Famous all over the county for her riding and jumping? Broke her back at a water-jump, and lay crippled for forty years. . . . Oh, dear, let us turn the page.

Here we have bustles. Your mother? Now, that is *really* the swan period. What a bend! The Grecian bend, was it not? The Greeks were first with everything, of course; but I do not recall this bend in any of their statues. Perhaps they could not hold it long enough to be sculptured. Of course, it is not *altogether* genuine; the bustle helped. But how adorable! How sorry your mother must have been when she had to go into those horrible clothes of the nineties, puff-sleeved jackets (by the way, I see they are in again; strange how even the worst things always come round) and stiff collars and sailor hats—yes, there she is in them.

And your Aunt Elizabeth, in a college group wearing large cricket pads—Newnham, is it? What year? 1890. Well, of course Newnham had been going for about twenty years then. . . . It was quite the thing to go to college, I suppose; now it seems to be less thought of, to be considered no use for getting jobs. I dare say your Aunt Elizabeth didn't have to think about jobs. Became a doctor, did she? I never knew Mrs. Robinson had been a doctor; why did she give it up? She left six forceps in? But that's nothing, surely. . . . Oh, all in the same wound; yes, I suppose that *would* be rather many. . . . *And* three swabs? Well, I dare say her mind was on cricket. It may happen to anyone, they say. Most people who have ever had an operation are simply full of forceps and swabs, I believe; they think it is rheumatism or neuritis. . . . It is wonderful, I often think, what additions, as well as subtractions, the human frame can stand. I suppose really we are put together *quite* at random, and a few objects more or less make very little difference; though I must say, when you see a picture of our insides, you wonder where extra forceps and swabs would go. But of course, they take the place of whatever the surgeon has just taken away, I forgot that. . . . Well, perhaps your Aunt Elizabeth was right; she goes in for chickens now, doesn't she?

You as a child; how pretty. How people change; still, I would know you anywhere. Quite in the nude. That has the advantage that you can't be dated by your clothes. Your school lacrosse team . . . and your first dance dress. Empire style. Clothes were pretty that year; nice high waists and simple lines.

But let us turn back to the Victorians. They fascinate me. There is a *je ne sais quoi* about them, a subtlety; they might have strange experiences, commit strange deeds, and say nothing. They are proud, reserved, self-contained. Your Aunt Geraldine looks like a mermaid, your Uncle Frank, behind his moustaches, seems to brood on strange lands. Had to leave the country suddenly? That would account for it, I suppose. Poor Uncle Frank. Did he have to be long away?

It was hushed up? That always takes a little time, of course. And then Uncle Frank came home, and married a Miss Jones. Had to leave the country *again*? What bad luck he had! Now-a-days, they seem to manage better, without so much travelling. Was he long abroad the second time? Always? Dear me. Yes, I see, this is his *hacienda* in the Argentine, with himself and Miss Jones, grown nice and plump, in the porch. . . . Oh, not Miss Jones? She stayed in England, with the children? Then this would be some other lady, more of the Argentine type. . . . I expect your uncle Frank was wise to settle there, among cattle; as your Aunt Elizabeth was wise to settle among chickens. Animals are a great resource. And so much nicer to rear them than to go and shoot them.

Photographs of ancestors are really much more interesting than the paintings of them they had before, because the camera cannot lie, so we know that they really did look like that. Now-a-days they touch them up more; the camera has learnt to lie. Besides, do we look as interesting? I am sure we do not. I could look at our ancestors for ever. Thank you so much for showing me yours. It has been a charming evening. You must come and see mine.

A charming evening. But as I drive home, the small cold wind of mortality hums round me with sighing breath. The way to dusty death seems to stretch before me, lit by those fading yellow oblongs wherefrom someone's ancestors gaze, pale pasteboard prisoners, to be wondered about, recalled, lightly summed and dismissed by us as we turn a page. So too shall we gaze out some autumn evening, prisoned and defenceless, to stir in posterity a passing idle speculation, a moment's memory. That? Oh, that is great-aunt Rose. . . . She wrote. Oh, nothing you would have heard of; I don't think she was ever much read, even at the time; she just wrote. Novels, essays, verse—I forget what else; she just wrote away, as those Georgians did. Rather dull, I think. What besides? Well, I think she just went about; nothing special. There *was* some story . . . but it's all so long ago, I've forgotten. She ended poor, having outlived whatever market she had, poor old thing. Yes, she went on writing, but no one read her . . . she died poor, killed, I think, in an aeroplane smash; she learnt to pilot too old; she should have stuck to motoring. But she would learn to fly, and finally smashed a friend's plane and herself . . . silly, really. She had grown very tiresome before the end, they say. But look, here is someone more interesting. . . .

It will be posterity's charming evening then, and theirs to pity, if they will, their pasteboard prisoners, as I now pity Aunt Geraldine with her mermaid's face and form, Uncle Frank who had to leave home so suddenly and so frequently, Great-Aunt Helen, of the rogue's face and little feather, who fell at the water-jump sixty years ago, Grandpapa General, who rode back with the Light Brigade, Grandmama, who had to be so often locking and unlocking her stores, Aunt Elizabeth with her forceps and her chickens, Aunt Amy rippling so elegantly from the waist down and marrying the curate who wrote tracts about the East-ward Position. . . .

Poor figures I feel we shall most of us cut beside them, when the Albums shall imprison us too.

ARM-CHAIR

ARM-CHAIR

I love it, I love it, and who shall dare
To chide me for loving that old arm-chair?

So, A century ago, defiantly enquired Miss Eliza Cook. Already, obviously, the sour and scornful denigrators of this article of furniture were busy with their cheap sneers, which one can only surmise to be based on envy. If Miss Cook's question were answered, one would find that the sneerers at the arm-chair (and they are many, in these days) were men who do not possess such chairs. They may be smart, modern men, whose chairs have arms of steel. They may be poor men; who cannot, perhaps, afford arm-chairs; who, having purchased one, possibly, on the Pay-Way system ("we never mention money here, Mr. Everyman"), found it reft from them at the last owing to their too close adherence to this policy of reticent silence. They find themselves arm-chairless; they have to sit up straight on armless chairs, an embittering posture, or on the floor (an undignified one), or betake themselves to their clubs, where they find all the arm-chairs in chronic use by others, and are further embittered. So they sit down at one of the club writing-tables, on some hard, straight-backed seat, and, with a venomous eye roving round the room, proceed to write letters to newspapers about arm-chair critics, arm-chair pacifists, militarists, generals, reformers, statesmen, politicians, concert-goers, and the like. What they actually object to so strongly is arm-chair newspaper-sitters, who sit a clutch of journals as a hen sits eggs, without, for the most part, ever hatching out one of them, but if some callow chick of an idea should come cheeping out of the sitter's head and find its chirping way to public print, he is denounced by the arm-chairless as an arm-chair critic. Possibly such denunciations also come from civil servants and those who have to sit at office tables to do their stuff. These can ill bear that criticisms and suggestions about life and the world should be emitted by the comfortable, slugging it at ease in their arm-chairs, lolling and lounging, twiring through their long spy-glasses at the scene which they with such bland and indolent effrontery criticize. No wonder that we who thus loll and twire rouse the wrath of those who must twire without lolling, those who have to do the work, and are peppered with the lazy fire from our arm-chair pea-shooters.

But we, calm and reposeful sedilians, do not resent such abuse or such envious contempt. We know that we have the best of it; that the most intelligent, as well as the easiest and most agreeable, criticism is emitted from the commodious depths of the easy chair wherein, *tranquillo animo*, we lie coiled in peace. (I speak as a female: for I am aware that gentlemen do not coil, but rather lie extended; this human law seems to apply also to bed.) Thus extended or coiled in our chairs, we vie happiness (as Evelyn wrote to Cowley about garden life, a far less comfortable affair) in a thousand easy and sweet diversions—"not forgetting," added Mr. Evelyn, "the innocent toils which you cultivate, the leisure and the liberty, the books, the meditations, above all the learned and choice friendships which you enjoy. Who would not, like you, *cacher sa vie*?" And who could not *cacher* it with far more comfort in an arm-chair than in a garden? What happiness thus to

> *waste away*
> *In gentle inactivity the day!*

Many of us, like the gentleman Steele knew, "fell into that way at the University, where the Youth are too apt to be lulled into a State of such Tranquillity as prejudices 'em against the Bustle of that Worldly Business, for which this part of their Education should prepare 'em. As he could with the utmost Secrecy be Idle in his own Chamber he says he was for some Years irrecoverably sunk and immers'd in the Luxury of an Easy Chair, tho' at the same time, in the general Opinion, he passed for a hard Student."

Fortunate gentleman. But there was no reason but his own averseness from such a path why he should not have been, in fact, a hard student, however deeply sunk, and even immersed, in the luxury of his easy chair. Books can pile the floor around the chair; dictionaries, histories, works of divinity, philosophy and literature in all languages, can stand in the shelves within easy reach; pen and paper can lie on a table at hand, or slip down between the chair's cushions and its arms. In our arm-chairs we may join the mob of gentlemen who write with ease; wit can amble well, go easily; masterpieces can trickle elegantly and indolently from our pens; imagination, dandled, pampered and stalled, can rise on spread wings and soar above Helicon, galloping among the seven planets, the firmament, and the empyreal heaven. What noble periods we conceive and pen; what stark and majestic lines, the starker in that our recumbent forms are so delicately stretched at ease.

Or music visits us, belling and stroking the ambient air, filling our room with linkèd sweetness, or with pure and complicated harmonies. Sometimes it will come from the Queen's Hall. Almost one can see that great assembly of listeners, sitting upright on hard chairs, afraid to stir or cough, straining forward to miss no chord, tier above tier of intent faces and rigid forms. While I am hearing the same sounds, or as near as makes no matter, reclined at ease in a warm and book-lined room, able to turn a switch and dismiss the whole affair when it no longer pleases. Does a soprano break out, shrilly tearing the air to tatters with a trilling scream? I turn the switch; she is gone; she troubles me no more than for one anguished second; peace and my arm-chair lap me about once more, like cloth of fine velvet of Turkey.

But it is not necessary, just because one sits in an

arm-chair, to pass the noon of one's life, like the gentleman whose habits Steele deplored, "in the Solitude of a Monk and the Guilt of a Libertine." One may have company, either in another arm-chair, should they be so fortunate, or on some other kind of chair, or even on the floor. Let the company sit where it likes, or where it can. So long as I am in my arm-chair, I do not care where or how it sits. Conversation flows; what witty things we say; what creeds we demolish and erect, what characters and literatures dissect, what tales recount, what revolutions deprecate or predict, what hot battles fight, what conceits and fantastications fangle! We tire the stars with talking and send them down the sky; the stars, and the moon, and all the celestial bodies, for they have no arm-chairs, they wander, they labour, or they are fixed, all tiring conditions. But ourselves we do not tire, lying at ease in our chairs, nothing active or labouring but our tongues. Night, day, and the crystal spheres revolve about us; in our arm-chairs we shall for ever sit, triumphing over Death and Chance and thee, O Time.

But, alas, how rarely are they quite long enough in the seat!

ASTRONOMY

ASTRONOMY

THE sand is cool to our bare feet, for the first time since breakfast. The sudden night has encompassed sea and shore, and, though they still hold the day's warmth, the sand no longer burns. It is a night for astronomy, the moon unrisen, the clear purple heavens thick inlaid with patines of bright gold. Look at the stars! Look, look up at the skies! Oh, look at all the firefolk sitting in the air!

My father has set up the telescope, its three legs dug into soft sand, its questing proboscis peering inquisitively into the peculiar mysteries of the sky. We all look through it in turn, and see what we can see. We concern ourselves mainly with the major planets. We note that Mars is low and red, Venus brilliant, Jupiter enormous, Saturn triple-ringed and lackeyed by his myriad satellites, Mercury and Uranus negligible, Neptune not to be descried. (Or is not all this true of one night? Perhaps I confuse several.)

Then we spy on the fixed stars; we trace out the Great and Little Bears, find the Pole Star, the constellation of Cassopeia, the Great Square of Pegasus, Perseus and Andromeda, Capella and the Kids, the Pleiades, Sirius, Arcturus, Algol, Betelgeuze, Orion and his belt. But Aldebaran, Cygnus, Vega, Rigel, and a

33

myriad more, I cannot, I am sure, identify. Can my father? Presumably, since he is, says our cook, "proprio come il Signor Iddio, che sa tutto, tutto." Alas, we are not like that. I perceive the heavenly bodies with the greatest difficulty: I lack siderial talent, with so much other. Still, I can find, after some search, the Bears and the Pole Star. For the rest, I say, with M. de Fontenelle's Countess, I will believe of the stars all you would have me.

And look, the Milky Way! Even I can find that, with my naked eye. "I wish you had a glass," says M. de Fontenelle, agreeing with my father, "to see this ant-hill of stars, this cluster of worlds, if I may so call 'em. They are in some sort like the Maldivian Islands: those twelve thousand banks of sand, separated by narrow channels of the sea, which a man may leap as easily as over a ditch. So near together are the vortexes of the Milky Way, that the people in one world may talk and shake hands with those of another; at least I believe the birds of one world may easily fly into another, and that pigeons may be trained up to carry letters, as they do in the Levant." This seems very probable, when one gazes up into that pale and beamy stream.

"The Galaxy," says my father. "From milk in Greek."

How many stars in the Galaxy? No one knows; no one has counted.

Why not?

For one thing, they are not all visible.

Not even with the strongest telescope in the world, aren't they visible?

But my father is occupied with Sirius.

Suppose one discovered a new star? New stars are born, every now and then. *The Story of the Heavens* says so. Suppose one should find a little new star, just, just hatched, like a fluffy yellow chick thrashing out of its egg. . . .

Father, what would you do if you saw a quite new star?

But my father, a modest man, whose profession is not astronomy, says that he would not know it for a new star.

Would Uncle Willie know a new star?

Probably.

Well, what would Uncle Willie do if he found a new star?

But my father is concerned with Jupiter and his satellites.

Venus slides, glittering and bland, down the sky to her bed.

A bright swoop down the western sky; a star shoots down, like Lucifer from heaven, and plunges into the dark horizon of the sea, to join the floating lights that mark the fishing-boats and the phosphorescent shoals that spark in their wake. Look, look, a falling star! Has it fallen into the sea? Did it make a great splash where it fell? Would it sink a ship, if it fell on it?

No, stars do not fall into the sea, nor anywhere on earth. They career through space.

But they *might* hit the earth, mightn't they?

My father replies that this would be unfortunate.

Well, what would happen? Would it set us on fire? Would it kill us?

But my father is occupied with Saturn and his rings.

My mother once said that the great boulders of rock strewn about all up the bed of the river Teiro might be bits of fallen stars. My mother told us very interesting and wonderful things. She said that the white promontory of Spezia, which, on a clear day, we could see east of the Gulf of Genoa, was marble mountains. If we were to ask *her* what would happen if a whole star hit the earth, we should have a tremendous blaze and conflagration in a minute.

The moon is coming, cries someone; and, sure enough, a rose-gold haze flushes the eastern horizon, heralding the golden rim, like the segment of an orange, that will rise and rise from the dark sea until it is a whole orange climbing up the sky, to flood the night and dim the stars. My father quotes Ben Jonson, who was so wrong about Hesperus entreating the moon's light, for how should one of the sun's goddess lovers entreat the advent of another, who must dim her?

But, for our part, we welcome the moon, swinging up among silver flames, flinging her golden causeway across the bay to the ripples at our feet.

Astronomy is over. Like the monkeys and marmosets of whom Mutianus tells, we hop and dance beneath the moon. A pig chase, we cry: for this pastime always concludes our astronomy. We race and chase about the brightening shore, up and down between the garden and the sea, in and out of the ripples that now glow gold as they curvet and spark, splashing lightly on damp sand. We flee and chase until we are as hot as if the moon were the sun, until we have no more breath to chase with or to flee.

At chasing and fleeing, I am as good as the next man; it is one of my stronger points. But deep in my heart there lies a shame; I am always the last to discern the Pole Star and the Bears. And sometimes I say that I see them without conviction, and fear, uneasily, that this may be an Untruth. Do the others really see these heavenly constellations as quickly as they make out?

BAKERY IN THE NIGHT

BAKERY IN THE NIGHT

How sweet a waft of warm bakery breathes up from the nether world below the pavement, as I pass the baker's at midnight! All night they are at it, it would seem, making and baking that doughy substance which smells so much better in the making than ever it tastes when made. Fried fish is otherwise; it tastes good, but smells terrible when frying. That is one of the things about fish; it always smells ill—fishy, in fact—but tastes good, and not fishy at all. There would be few ichthyophagi if we judged fishes by their smell. Some bold and hungry experimenter must have ventured long since to disregard the fishy savour and try it in the mouth; he was rewarded, justified, and the tradition was established. The same with meat. But bread, poor enough stuff in the mouth, is delicious, when preparing, to the nose. Unfortunately this wears off after baking, and a fresh loaf smells of nothing in particular, while a stale one smells of mould.

But so delicious is this warm and bready odour that breathes up through a grating in the pavement that I pause entranced to sniff. For a moment I am persuaded that the bread I shall eat to-morrow will taste like this celestial smell; it will be manna, not mere bread. Nay, it will be ambrosia, such as is heaped on the tables of gods; it will be food for angels, for gourmets, for Lucullus at his solitary suppers. The sweet yeasty fragrance steals on the night, lingering on the air like the gentlest pretty insinuating tune. No wonder that men have sold their bodies and their souls for bread, if this is what bread is. Bread and circus games—the Romans were right in demanding these, in feeling that, together, they made the adequate life.

But, as I stand there and smell, strange unwelcome stories recur to my memory, of how bakers make bread. Has it not been said that, if we should watch them at it, bread-consumption would slump down, the staff of life would bend under us, and we should have recourse to potatoes and cabbage, rice, and even sago? It is the same, of course, with jam, with sausages, with veal. Better see no food prepared. Close the eyes, open the mouth, and say a grace that you were not there at the making of the pleasant finished product that slips so agreeably down your throat and into your system. And, if you come to that, what would your system look like, do you suppose, if you should have the misfortune to see *that*? It ill behoves us, with our insides, to be dainty about looking upon the manufacture of anything that goes into them; at its worst stage the object to be consumed can scarcely have presented so ill an appearance as does the place prepared for its reception.

BATHING

BATHING

1. *Off the Florida Keys*

OVER the pale jade-green shallows, a tiny breeze runs, ruffling the surface of the Florida Straits into ribbed glass, setting little ripples slapping against the man-grove-grown clumps of earth that enisle these strange seas. You may wade a mile out from the white beach, palm-fringed, of the Keys; wade towards Havana, ankle-deep, knee-deep, thigh-deep, waist-deep, breast-deep. Can one wade right across the straits to Cuba or Havana? I do not know: evening falls, and I have reached neither. Evening falls, and the sea, sunset-drenched, glows from green to rose, like gardens of ripening fruit beneath a glass roof. On the ribbed floor of sand gleam the coral forests: I stoop and break off brittle twigs and branches and flowers, as one gathers mushrooms or raspberries in a field. Through the forests dart slippery fishes, silver, coral and turquoise, or striped black like little zebras; they glance through my hands. Here is a tiny goblin being in gleaming blue, with horns and a hump and goggling eyes; it is not fleet enough, and I cup it between my hands, and guide it to the nearest island, scoop a hole for it in the sand and fill it with water; it swims round and round, goblin eyes seeking escape; it feels its position acutely; it must be turned adrift again into the Florida seas, to join its goblin kind.

The boat that lies tethered to a mangrove tree on one of the islands is unmoored; one rows her back, while the others wade beside, shoving her over the sandy shallows, to beach her on the palm-fringed Key, where the evening breeze goes rustling among the star-shaped heads of slender, leaning royal palms, and the small waves shuffle sighing on white sand.

It has been a lovely bathe, an exquisite wade, an immersion, however partial, in enchanted waters. Nevertheless, of all the world's uneasy beds on which to tread, on which to sit, a bed of coral is the least deserving of that name. Of what is the marine cœlenterate polyps thinking, that he builds him of the skeletons of his tribe such harsh, such jagged arborescent beds for his habitation?

> *Rise, rise, and heave thy rosie head*
> *From thy coral-pav'n bed. . . .*

One is happy to know that the spirit was here mistaken, and that dear Sabrina, sitting under the glassy, cool, translucent wave of the Severn, was not sitting on coral, nor, as his excited fancy elsewhere tries to make out, on diamond rocks. We may be sure that Sabrina's bed and seats were of Severn mud, and fortunate she was that this was so. She would have said, I think, with Clive, and with all who have waded sandal-less off the Florida Keys, "I have no desire for coral."

2. *Off the Ligurian Coast*

The sea's warm edge sways lisping on hot sand, curling into tiny ripples, hissing, creaming, running delicately back. Wade in, take five steps in water as warm as a tepid bath, and the sharply shelving beach fails beneath your feet and leaves you swimming. Lapped in the clear, thin stuff, so blue, so buoyant, so serene, you can conceive no reason for ever leaving it. Strange element, on which you may lie stretched full length as on a bed, eyes closed, the sun hot on your face, wriggling your spread hands now and then like fins to propel you; or you may stand upright with folded arms, treading the sea with your feet; or hurl yourself through the water arm over arm; or dive down to the bottom of the deep, gather a handful of seaweed or pebbles, and shoot up. You may start swimming out to sea, heading for Corsica; swim and swim, until you are suddenly afraid you will meet a shark, and turn and race panicking for shore. Yes, there have been sharks in our bay; we have never met one, but we sometimes fear that we may.

Often we take out the canoe when we bathe. Three sit in the middle and one on each end, when it capsizes, we ride astride on its backside. Oh, pleasure, reeling goddess, I have spent much time with you, but I think that while bathing of an August afternoon in our bay with the canoe, we know you at your most reeling, your most zoneless. Such felicity seems to know no limit; measureless to man, it seems the pleasure of some celestial state, in which we swim and sport in the blue and heavenly inane, like the *putti* that leap through wreaths of flowers upon a painted ceiling.

Such pleasure, I say, like the pleasures of paradise, should know no term; it should endure for ever. But to our bathing a term is set. Unlike the children of the Italian *bagnanti*, we are summoned from the sea. We leave that lovely, that clear and celestial element, for thin air quivering with heat.

3. *In the Cam*

The birds wake me; many minds with but a single thought, they all break out singing at once; one does not know why. They wake me; they would wake the dead, if the dead lay where I lie, in an open arbour in a little wood by the river's edge. The river, pale and secret, slides past, between the green shadow of willows and the grey light of dawn and the white shining of the hanging may-bushes and the deep green of the waving weeds. It flows towards Cambridge, but will be long, at this rate, in arriving at that learned town, for it scarcely seems to move. Sluggishly the weeds wave, and with them the gold and white chalices with their broad-leafed saucers. A phantom stream, a pale dream of green shadow and grey light. Alone in the dawn world, a pink climbing rose gives colour, a pure sharp note in a faint chromotone of greys.

The east too grows rose-pink, beyond the grey pricks of the willow leaves. Drowsily I lie, and watch the sun rise to the clamour of the birds. When it looks above the pollarded head of the large willow on the opposite bank, I shall bathe.

The river emerges from greyness into deep green colour and clear light. The sun tops the pollard. I throw off blankets and night clothes and slip from the bank into the cold stream. Spreading my arms wide, I let the slow flow carry me gently along through shadow and light, between long weedy strands that slimily embrace me as I drift by, between the bobbing white and gold cups and slippery juicy stems, beneath willows that brush my head with light leaves, beneath banks massed high with may, smelling sharp and sweet above the musky fragrance of the tall cow-parsley. Buttercup fields shine beyond those white banks; the chestnuts lift their candles high against the morning sky.

But suddenly there sprung,
A confident report, that through the country rung,
That Cam *her daintiest flood, long since entituled*
　　Grant . . .
Is sallying on for Ouze, *determin'd by the way*
To entertain her friends the Muses with a lay.
Wherefore to show herself ere she to Cambridge *came,*
Most worthy of that town to which she gives the
　　name,
Takes in her second head, from Linton *coming in,*

By Shelford *having slid, which straightway she doth*
>   *win;*
Than which a purer stream, a delicater brook,
Bright Phœbus *in his course doth scarcely overlook.*
Thus furnishing her banks, as sweetly ,she doth glide
Towards Cambridge, *with rich meads laid forth on*
>   *either side;*
And with the Muses oft did by the way converse . . .
A wondrous learned flood. . . .

Possibly. But possibly also, by the mud of three centuries, a less pure stream, a less delicate brook now
than then.

Beneath a hanging may-tree, a thin cheeping comes;
a brood of baby moor-chicks has hatched in the night,
and now swims out to explore the green and gold
world, four small black balls behind their mother,
chirping their excitement to the morning.

I splash up stream against the flowing weeds, scram-
ble out and dry myself. The pure stream, the delicate
brook, the learned flood, has a floor of soft mud, and
is cold before the sun is high. I creep again into
blankets, and would sleep the day in, but for the in-
defatigably cantiferous birds.

BED

BED

1. *Getting into it*

WHEN I consider how, in a human creature's normal life, each day, however long, however short, however weary, however merry, circumstanced by whatever disconcerting, extravagant, or revolting chances of destiny, ends in getting into bed—when I consider this, I wonder why each day is not a happy, hopeful, and triumphant march towards this delicious goal; why, when the sun downs and the evening hours run on, our hearts do not lighten and sing in the sure and certain hope of this recumbent bliss. If it were a bliss less recurrent, more rare and strange, its exquisite luxury would surely seem a conception for the immortal gods, beyond any man's deserts. Even through the cold and sober definition given by the dictionary, comfort and anticipation warmly throb. "It consists for the most part of a sack or mattress of sufficient size, stuffed with something soft or springy, raised generally upon a 'bed-stead' or support, and covered with sheets, blankets, etc., for the purpose of warmth. The name is given both to the whole structure in its most elaborate form, and, as in 'feather-bed,' to the stuffed sack or mattress which constitutes its essential part. (A person is said to be *in bed*, when undressed and covered with the bedclothes)."

What delicious memories and hopes do the quiet words evoke! A sack or mattress of sufficient size, stuffed with something soft or springy, raised generally upon a bed-stead or support, and covered with sheets, blankets, etc., for the purpose of warmth. Can well-being further go? Yes: for the purpose of even greater warmth, there may be a rubber bottle filled with hot water. Reflecting on, and still more, experiencing, this state of Olympian, of almost lascivious pleasure, how one pities Titania sleeping sometime of the night on her bank among thyme, oxlips, violets and snakes, her only coverlet the cast skins of these reptiles, which serve us not for sheets but for shoes. She was but a fairy queen, and knew nothing of our soft human elaborations of comfort. "Thou shalt lie in a bed stuffed with turtle's feathers; swoon in perfumed linen, like the fellow was smothered in roses."

And to your more bewitching, see, the proud
Plumpe Bed beare up, and swelling like a cloud. . . .
. . . Throw, throw
Your selves into the mighty over-flow
Of that white Pride, and Drowne
The night, with you, in floods of Downe. . . .

That is better than the bank where the wild thyme grows; better, even, almost certainly, than the bed which Eve made out of flowers in the blissful nuptial bower, or than the roses that smothered the fellow. Not that down is necessary, or even desirable: a good hair mattress over box springs is more resilient, and as accordant to the frame as one can wish. The down can fill the pillows. The sheets are of smooth, fine cambric; not linen, which is heavier, colder, and less pliable, even when perfumed. Blankets should be according to season and temperature; it is well to have one or two in reserve, cast back over the bed's foot.

Climb, then, into this paradise, this epicurism of pleasure, this pretty world of peace. Push up the pillows, that they support the head at an angle as you lie sideways, your book held in one hand, its edge resting on the pillow. On the bed-head is a bright light canopied by an orange shade; it illustrates the page with soft radiance, so that it shines out of the environing shadows like a good deed in a naughty world. You are reading, I would suggest, a novel; preferably a novel which excites you by its story, lightly titillating, but not furrowing, the surface of the brain. Not poetry; not history; not essays; not voyages; not biography, archæology, dictionaries, nor that peculiar literature which publishers call belles-lettres. These are for daytime reading; they are not somnifacient; they stimulate the mind, the æsthetic and appreciative faculties, the inventive imagination; in brief, they wake you up. You will never, I maintain, get to sleep on Shakespeare, Milton, or Marvell, or Hakluyt, or Boswell, or Montaigne, or Burton's *Anatomy*, or Sir Thomas Browne, or Herodotus, or any poetry or prose that fundamentally excites you by its beauty, or any work that imparts knowledge. These will light a hundred candles in your brain, startling it to vivid life. A story, and more particularly a story which you have not read before, will hold your attention gently on the page, leading it on from event to event, drowsily pleased to be involved in such fine adventures, which yet demand no thought. Let the story amuse, thrill, interest, delight, it matters not which; but let it not animate, stimulate or disturb, for sleep, that shy nightbird, must not be startled back as it hovers over you with drowsy wings, circling ever near and nearer, until its feathers brush your eyes, and the book dips suddenly in your hand. Lay it aside then; push out the light; the dark bed, like a gentle pool of water, receives you; you sink into its encompassing arms, floating down the wandering trail of a dream, as down some straying river that softly twists and slides through goblin lands, now dipping darkly into blind caves, now emerging, lit with the odd, phosphorescent light of oneiric reason, unsearchable and dark to waking eyes.

But what a small mischance can mar this clinic joy, this opulent bed of pleasure. Adam and Eve doubtless encountered pricks and thorns and crumpled leaves in their roseate couch, though we are reassured as to the completely unentomologous condition of the bridal bower. And our passible frames may meet, in some untended mattress, with a lump. Or, in some alien dwelling, beneath the roof-tree of callous friends, with coverings cold as charity, blankets scant and thin. The

eiderdown, if eiderdown there be, may glide and slide
to the floor, like a French *duvet*. The hot-bottle may
leak. Your head may face the window, and the cur-
tains be of white casement, with a gap between to
admit the dawn. The bird of dawning may sing all
night long. A clock may tick, and be too large to be
shut in the wardrobe. There may be a thin, transaudi-
ent wall, and a snorer beyond it. Or a snorer in your
very bed, or even a somniloquent. Worst of all, worse
than any other clinic grief, almost too profound a
grief to be so much as glanced at in a survey of pleasures, it is conceivable that the light may only be extinguishable by the door. I believe, nay, I assert with
confidence and deliberation, having clearly in mind all
other bedroom woes—such as hard mattress, flock pillows, scant covering, intrusive dawn, eoan bird-songs,
disappointed or fatiguing love, companions lapped and
chrysalised in robbed blankets and close-gripped
sheets, and yet turning and ever turning still—I say
with deliberation, that this is the shrewdest stroke of
fortune, the harshest bedroom chance, a light only
extinguishable by the door.

2. *Not getting out of it*

Infinite and interminable rivers of eloquence have
run, singing and murmuring on this inexhaustible
theme. It is probable that all has been said or sung on
it that can be sung or said. Yet one is bound to contribute one's tributary, one's little stream of eloquence,

to the flood which has flowed down the ages in praise of this great joy. The point is, once in the bed of pleasure, why get out of it? Humanity sees this point clearly every morning, yet, nearly every morning, obfuscates it, deserts the sheltering couch (where so much of the business of life might be transacted if we so chose, and at so much less cost of labour and distraction), and steps into the cold embattled world without.

How long wilt thou sleep, O sluggard? when wilt thou arise out of thy sleep? Yet a little sleep, a little slumber, a little folding of the hands to sleep. . . . Go to the ant, thou sluggard; consider her ways and be wise. . . .

Yes, but the ant's bed (even if the female ant does leave it as early in the morning as is here implied), is but a poor miserable resting-place compared with ours; the phrase "to seek repose on an ant-bed" has been used as a synonym of fantastic mischoice. We must not be surprised if ants rise betimes, instead of replying, as we do, to those who rouse them, "You have waked me too soon, I must slumber again." Do not praise the ant's ready exsuscitation, but pity rather that entomological barrenness of invention which has never furnished this hard-worked insect with a really comfortable bed. Not for the ant the drowsy exit from delicious dreams to a world of soft down, box springs, and sheets that gentlier lie than tired eyelids upon tired eyes. Not for her (or him) the lively cup that disperses the somniatory clouds from the brain, the clean newspaper hot from the press, discreetly waiting to unfold its strange matutinal tale, the pile of letters, each throbbing with its little human message, each shut behind its enveloping protecting veil, which need not be torn asunder until, or unless, we choose—not these for the ant, waking on her stinging heap to another busy, bustling, onerous, formicarian day. Unhappy insect, motion-obsessed, for ever dragging, fetching, carrying, from one site to another, objects which are very well where they are, like those porters in Paris stations who can let nothing lie . . . such labours she can scarcely begin too late in the day. Consider the ant's ways and be wise indeed, for her labour is like unto ours; we too are for ever dragging, fetching, carrying, changing, objects which are very well as they are . . . such labours we too can scarcely begin too late in the day. The advantage we have over the ant is that we know it; we have reason, she only instinct.

Lie back, then, among pillows and, gently yet firmly encouched, await the onslaught of the bellicose day, whose buffets jar less rudely those who take them lying down. Yield to the storm; venture not out into it, and it will pass.

> *Thou shalt have thy Caudles*
> *before thou dost arise:*
> *For churlishnesse breeds sicknesse*
> *and danger therin lies.*

Thus spoke a better lover than all those who have shouted to wake their ladies at dawn, calling them slug-a-beds, pigs in straw, bidding them rise and dress and come a-maying, asking them why should they sleep when they have slept enough (what a question!), and, worst of all, telling them that their breakfast stays until they are up—water-gruel, sugar-sops, brown ale, and toast. A kind lover or husband would bring all these to the bedroom; an intelligent one would be consuming them there himself. After this meal (unless quite incapacitated by its various ingredients), you may lie and reflect on all the occupations and works which man has pursued in bed; how Milton therein composed much of *Paradise Lost;* how Dido and her court feasted Æneas and his warriors, and after supper listened to his mournful travelogue, all reclining on their couches; how emperors and dictators have lain on beds while damsels danced before them and made music; how Sir John Suckling practised and perfected in bed that card-playing by which he lived; how Hobbes did mathematics, drawing lines on his thigh and on the sheets; how generals have planned victories and ordered attacks; how the Kings of France received their ministers in bed and dispensed affairs of state; how Lady Mary Wortley Montague received poets, and Prime Ministers the news of victories; how men are born in bed, and frequently die there; how Samuel Pepys lay late with great pleasure, and Samuel Johnson lay all his life until noon or until two, purposing to rise at eight and telling young men that nobody

who did not rise early would ever come to good.
Indeed, so much of the world's business has been performed in bed, that even to begin to consider it will
be a morning's work. Rise early and bed late, says a
foolish old adage, but does not explain why you will
be better out of bed than in. A thing too often forgotten is that, once you are out of it, you or someone else will have to make it. There was a certain
man named Æneas who had kept his bed eight years,
whom St. Peter bade arise, and added that he was to
make his bed. Æneas arose, and, we suppose, made his
bed; but, after eight years of lying in it, this daily rising and making it must have seemed very strange,
and we are not told how long it lasted.

Indeed, more should be done in bed than is (even
more). We spend too many of these precious clinic
hours in blind stupor, tenebrizing it like polar bears
in winter. Going to bed is a nocturnal pleasure; but
not getting out of it is a journal one, to be enjoyed
with all the innocent ardours and relish of the day.
Slug then in sloth, and languish in delights, while the
day breaks and shadows flee away.

But the luxury of pleasure is marred, as time creeps
on, by a bitter foreknowledge born of experience.
Sooner or later some one of those who are under your
roof, unless you have your roof all day to yourself,
will enquire if you are ill, and, if you are well, at what
hour you are proposing to rise. Why, in the name of
all the great bed-lovers, should I be ill because I prefer to remain in so charming a refuge as my bed? Did

Milton's daughters ask him if he was ill when he preferred to dictate from his bed? Was Dr. Johnson ill?
Were the French Kings? No, I am not ill; I am merely
philoclinic . . . that is my answer, if I can but make it
to her who arrives to clean my flat. . . .

BELIEVING

BELIEVING

Yes, I believe everything; you cannot tell me anything that I cannot believe.

That the forbidden fruit of Paradise was an apple presents no difficulties to me; nor that mermaids sing when combing their hair and swans when dying, that ostriches eat keys and a whale ate Jonah, that a remora can stay a ship, and the cockatrice, who is hatched by a toad out of the egg of a cock, slay a man by a glance.

All the reputed strange habits of birds and beasts I believe, even that little birds tell tales, unicorns love virgins, dragons are the faithfullest of pets, wild horses the most inquisitive, and yet the most uninformed, of quadrupeds, who still stick at nothing to drag secrets from people, but always drag in vain.

I believe (can you?) that

> *Slow* Boötes *underneath him sees*
> *In th'icy* Isles, *those Goslings hatcht of Trees;*
> *Whose fruitfull leaves, falling into the Water,*
> *Are turn'd (they say) to living Fowls soon after;*

and that

> *Rotten sides of broken Ships do change*
> *To* Barnacles; *O Transformation strange!*

65

'Twas first a green Tree, then a gallant Hull,
Lately a Mushroom, now a flying Gull.

And I believe in dowsing, and that anyone can divine water anywhere, whether it is there or not.

I believe in the Athanasian Trinity, and in angels; angels in heaven, on earth, and in the midmost air; angels with flaming swords expelling our parents from Paradise and obstructing Balaam's ass; French angels assisting the Allied armies at Mons and turning back General Von Kluck's march on Paris; Ulster angels crowding about Derry; Thomist angels crowding on needles; weeping angels distressed at what they see; guardian or tutelary angels steering our wayward course.

I believe that most things move the underjaw when eating, the crocodile not; that sirloins were knighted by an English king; that Diogenes lived in a tub, St. Simon Stylites on a pillar, chameleons on air, salamanders in fire, mermen in the sea; that corpses bleed when their murderer approaches; that what I read in the newspapers is true.

I can be every man's gull, and am infinitely persuadable. For to believe greatly is to enlarge life's oddity; to teratologize and credit strange relations, to run open-mouthed after aniles, or old wives' tales, illustrates the world with coloured candles, whose queer and flickering flames quaver into dim hidden corners, suggesting the goblin tenebrios that lurk therein, defining little but denying nothing. The clear and garish lucence of the sceptical spirit I utterly reject: it is so dull.

> *And there is nothing left remarkable*
> *Beneath the visiting moon.* . . .

That is what it ends in.

Give me a loud lie. Give me "misse-stories, hisse-stories, by the old Serpent hissed and buzzed among superstitious men"; give me "that babbling and fabling Abdias," who can tell me Ethiopian fables, and entertain me "in a fools' Paradise situate above the highest mountains, with such delicacies as shew that Adam's children are still in love with the forbidden fruit."

I promise you I will swallow all you give me, I will reject nothing, I will not strain at gnats, no, nor at camels neither. He over there, you say he is a were-wolf, and prowls howling by night over Primrose Hill? I can well believe it; he has that air. That other, he is a spy for the Russian government, and that is where he gets all his money from. He instigates strikes; his pockets bulge with Russian gold. There are some Nazi spies here too; they track down and murder refugees. As for that group over there, they indulge in the wildest, the oddest debauches—you would scarcely believe if I should tell you. Yes, I can believe, but you could not. . . . I can even believe that traveller from Bavaria, who last week saw a beautiful young man transformed into a goat.

I should like to sit in a coffee-house; one used to

hear, from all accounts, the most ridiculous tales there. Everything was largened out of all reason and likelihood, like a flea under a magnifying glass, becoming thereby worthy of credence. But coffee-houses have degenerated, they are used now for rapid meals, and there is less time for tales. I am told that they still tell fine tales in taverns, and that after a short time in a tavern, a man can believe anything. Yes, but I do not need taverns; I can believe anything on tomato-juice.

It is good to believe so much. The only drawback is that I never have that fine truculent moment when I say to my informant, "You lie."

BIRD IN THE BOX

BIRD IN THE BOX

HE LIVES in elegant retirement in a house of dark tor-
toise-shell, behind an oval china door on which is
painted a blue lake, a blue and pink sky, three transparent pink mountains, a rocky shore, three red-roofed
houses, three slim bending trees, and two sailing-boats.
A small lake paradise, you think, and wonder what it
does there, so sweetly, gaily set in shining gold-flecked
dark-umber shell. Then you lightly touch a spring,
and lo, a miracle. The door of lake and mountains
springs back, opening wide, revealing its inner side,
on which winds a broad reach of blue water (lake or
river?) with more pink mountains, more small red-
roofed houses on the shore. This tiny china land and
waterscape springs up from over a golden floor, a
broidered mesh of woven flowers and leaves, like one
of those enflowered golden meads in Paradise where,
it is said, the blessed saints walk in bliss; and simul-
taneously there rises from this shining bed a bird. You
will not credit this most extravagant sight, and I myself, as Herodotus was wont to say, am slow to believe it, but it is, nevertheless, the truth. An iridescent
bird, a bird of shining blue and green, peacock-hued,
tiny, he springs up, he flaps blue wings, he opens a
small beak, he sings, turning this way and that, like a

prima donna, against the oval background of pink mountains and blue lake. A stream, a fountain, of sweet pure lovely shrillness cascades into the air, unearthly, celestial, like the songs of angels which the blessed saints, walking on the golden floor, doubtless hear. This (approximately) is the tune that he sings[1]:

And, having sung it, folds his wings and retires, lying suddenly, swiftly down on his side on the golden meadow, which opens to receive his small form, and the china door snaps shut on gold-broidered floor and vanished bird. The sweet echo of that piping cadence still lilts upon the silent air; I hold in my hand a mute shell box, dark umber, flecked with gold, inset with an oval door, the outside of a closed door, whereon blue lake and transparent pink mountains and slim trees delicately smile, lying firmly, reticently, over the strange secret within, over music fallen dumb and a blue bird sunk asleep beneath a flowery golden floor.

---

[1] My thanks are due to Miss Livia Gollancz, who patiently and skilfully took down this tune straight from the bird's beak—no easy task, with so rapid a performer.

A bird of pleasure indeed. Like Walton's nightingale, he breathes such sweet music out of his little instrumental throat, that it might make mankind to think miracles are not ceased. He that at midnight (when the very labourer sleeps securely) should hear (as I have very often) the clear airs, the sweet descant, the natural rising and falling, the doubling and redoubling of his voice, might well be lifted above earth, and say, Lord, what music hast thou provided for the Saints in Heaven, when thou affordest men such music on earth! And this makes me (as it made Walton) the less to wonder at the many aviaries in Italy.

So much for the bird of pleasure, of which very much more might be said. In brief, how infinitely am I taken with this agreeable cheat! Like the phœnix, like the sun, he sinks into his golden bed only to rise again. Call him, and he will return, singing his carol before his opened door, turning this way and that, with flirting wings, against china lake and hills—tirra lirra sweet sweet sweet!

But will there come a day when he does not come, when, though his door springs back, his gold bed holds him still asleep and stirless beneath its starry mesh? Or a day when he cannot get back, when, his song ended, he still stands poised as for flight, lacking power to fall sideways and sink into the floor, so that the little door shuts on him and crushes him as he stands? For at times he seems weaker, more tardy in his retreat, and you may glimpse him lying half sunk in gold, with the china lakescape resting lightly on his folded blue wing. Are he and the spell that bids him come and go immortal, or will the enchantment one day end, and leave only a box of dark and shining shell, with china door closed tightly over a golden mesh and a buried, songless bird?

Come, press the spring once more; make sure that he will come. Rustle, flutter, tirra lirra sweet!

BOOK AUCTIONS

BOOK AUCTIONS

IT IS a singular scene. Around the room sit and stand inner and outer circles of impassive men; each holds a catalogue, each a pencil. Another and still more impassive man enters, every few minutes, into the middle of the circle, holding up, for their critical, sophisticated and supercilious stare, a book. None of them, it is apparent, think much of this book; it is, in each case, to judge from their expressions, a book that ought to go pretty cheap, a defective book, a book that, if they purchase it, will stand on their shelves unsold for ever. Sometimes it is several books; a lot: all poor.

Only one man in the room admires and likes these books; he is the presiding god, raised above the rest on a dais. He thinks very well of all the books; he likes books; he is a bibliophile, a bibliolater, even a bibliomaniac. He is, in brief, a bibliopole. He too, has an impassive face, but you can tell by his voice and his utterances that he likes books. He must feel lonely, presiding over this gathering of bored bibliophobes. Yet he conceals it; he addresses them in dulcet, persuasive accents, though not infrequently his tone gently conveys admonition and reproof, a kindly but shocked, "Come, come, my dear sirs! Only five pounds for this admirable work! Come now, we all know better than that!" But he does not say it; except by the inflexions of his admirably modulated voice. Ever so slightly turning towards some unresponsive gentleman in the circle, he says, "Guineas. Five guineas bid." After that, with other slight glances round, "Five ten. I am bid five pounds ten. Fifteen. Six Pounds. Guineas. Six ten, I am bid. . . ."

As he speaks, his eyes turn to and fro, from one to another, as if he watched tennis. But none but he has spoken; none but he, one would say, has moved. By what silent telepathy has he divined from them their offers of these shillings of which he makes mention? Or does he invent them? Is he hypnotising these hard bibliophobes with his gentle, even tones, uttering his own hopes and counsels, like the still small voice of conscience in their ears, so that when at length he pauses, (why he ever stops, is not known; since he never gets any response, it cannot be that the moment arrives when he gets less response than before) when he at last breaks off, and murmurs that the book in question has been sold to such an one, for such a price, the individual mentioned accepts his destiny, half believing that he has indeed offered this preposterous sum for a book which he dislikes and despises. That little motion he made with his catalogue; the time he sucked his pencil; scratched his chin; blew his nose; twirled his moustache; jerked his head; crossed his legs; winked his eyes; performed any one of those thousand little actions by which humankind reacts to the encompassing universe; these must have committed him to this purchase, involved him in the payment of this sum so far in excess of the value of the book, or the lot of books, which seems to have passed into his possession.

Very well. Life is like that. He must accept his portion, and sell it, if he can, at a price a little more than that which he has given, if only he can meet a fool.

Thus (I imagine) these silent book merchants cogitate, as the books are, one after another, inexplicably knocked down to them.

Alternatively, have they actually intended, by the trifling nods and becks that have escaped them, to convey to him who can read their very thoughts the little advances which have mounted to such a sum? If so, it shows once more the perils of competition. The delirious excitement of rivalry which stimulates the horse to run ahead of the horse in front of him, stirs in the blood of these hard-bitten men, egging them on to offer, in emulous rage, sums which they never in cold blood would have paid over any counter. "Ten shillings," says (or indicates) Mr. Robinson; "fifteen," the prompt repartee is hurled back by the flirt of Mr. Smith's catalogue; "twenty," Mr. Robinson, now roused, tilts his chair to convey; and "guinea," replies Mr. Smith's tilted hat. And so on and higher, in dumb but heated emulation, until one or other of the agonists comes to himself shaking his head as one who emerges from some strange delirious dream, and the disappointed, though calm, agonarch awards the prize to his rival.

Meanwhile, while these contests of giants rage about me, I sit rigid and stirless, benumbed, beclumpsed and dull. I dare not move nor breathe, nor lift my eye to encounter, perhaps, that roving eye which is so extreme to mark the least motion, so alert to interpret it. There is a book I should like to buy, but it is not due yet; we are only at number 532, which is called *Coleoptera of the British Islands*, and should I but uncross my knees, it would be mine, in five volumes, with coloured plates. They have reached twelve and sixpence. "Anyone bid fifteen?" That commanding, probing glance passes over me.

> *My nerves are all chain'd up in Alabaster,*
> *And I a statue; or as* Daphne *was*
> *Root-bound, that fled* Apollo.
> *Fool, do not boast,*
> *Thou canst not touch the freedom of my minde*
> *With all thy charms. . . .*

"Fifteen. I am bid fifteen" . . . By me? Quite possibly . . . no, he looks elsewhere; the *Coleoptera* are knocked down to a booseller on whose shelves I shall triumphantly see its five volumes, its coloured plates, reposing in unwanted redundance, because that unguarded bookseller coughed at the crucial moment.

Off they go again. "Five shillings bid. . . . Seven and six." . . . What is this? The enquiring eye is on me;

I realise that I have hiccupped. "Ten . . . twelve and six. . . ." Someone else must have hiccupped too, for the eye passes to and fro between me and another; the thing has become a rally. I have hiccupped again; that makes fifteen shillings. Seventeen and six, twenty . . . my colleague in distress must be cured, for he does not raise my last. "Twenty. I am bid twenty shillings. . . ." I shake my head, in denial of this assertion; it is useless. "Twenty shillings I am bid. . . . Sold for twenty shillings." The book is mine; I look at my catalogue and see that it is a French book about Venus. . . . Yes, and about Eunuchs too. . . . Quite definitely I cannot, no, I will not take it home; I will explain to the clerk afterwards. . . .

The auction proceeds. Soon it will reach my book—the *Bucaniers of America,* 3rd edition, 1704. How greatly I desire it! Surely I can win it, seeing that, despite all my struggles not to do so, I won Venus and the Eunuchs.

"640." It is held up before us; I see its stained title page; felix culpa, fortunate stain, that will keep it within my means. "Fifteen shillings," says the auctioneer. My hiccup was cured, apparently, by the shock of acquiring Venus, but I flick my catalogue, meaning "Seventeen and six." What is this? He does not see me; he looks towards some haggling bookseller who has blown his nose; he says, "seventeen and six," but not to me. I too blow my nose; the word is now "One pound," but it is the word of the dumb Mr. Robinson, who has tilted his bowler hat to the left.

"Guinea," I mutely cry, flapping my catalogue like a signal of distress. He will not look, he passes by; he observes Mr. Jones to scratch his cheek, and says "Twenty-five." I am as a desperate castaway on a lone island, signalling vainly to ships that steam unheeding by, picking up other castaways from other islands, but never me. In vain I flap my catalogue, cough, clear my throat, cross and uncross my legs, jerk my chin. The *Bucaniers* are flung to and from between Mr. Jones and Mr. Robinson in mute, tense rally and return. "Thirty. I am bid thirty . . ." Mr. Jones is slackening; he performs no more little actions; he slumps in his chair; the game is to Mr. Robinson. I cannot endure it; I spring to my feet. That chaste and muted hall is rent by a cry. "Two pounds."

The crude and raucous vocality of my bid shocks the mute multitude to surprise. The auctioneer at last looks my way; impassively he murmurs, "I am bid two pounds. Going for two pounds." He rakes Messrs. Robinson and Jones with enquiring eyes; he decides that their gestures are those of bored negation; they have lost interest in the *Bucaniers*, and are thinking about something else.

"Sold for two pounds."

The *Bucaniers* are mine.

But I should have said thirty-five. The *Bucaniers* were not mounting by ten shilling steps. The delirium of auctions turns the brain.

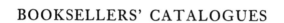

BOOKSELLERS' CATALOGUES

BOOKSELLERS' CATALOGUES

How lightly, softly, insinuatingly, they arrive, flipping
through the letterbox, alighting like leaves on the
passage floor; green like leaves of spring, red or brown
or orange like leaves of autumn, or white like drifts
of snow; but each folded neatly and precisely in a
wrapper of thin or stout dun-coloured paper. I will
not open them; I will not slit that concealing jacket
that protects me from the song of these luring sirens;
like Odysseus and his sailors, I will be deaf and blind.
I will cast them, as I cast without a pang all the other
catalogues of merchandise that arrive in my home, un-
opened into the waste-paper basket.

That small, orange-red being, the colour of a street
beacon, in its stout paper jacket—I gather it up to fling
it into the basket. Two inches of orange-hued catalogue protrude from each end of the wrapper, closely
printed; odd, how booksellers seem always short of
paper, so that they have to use every inch of even
the covers of their catalogues for their lists of wares.
What shows on the two inches of double column visible above the wrapper is:

1063 [**Utterson** (E. N.)] Se-
lect Pieces of Early Popular
Poetry: re-published prin-
cipally from Early Printed

Copies, in the Black Letter,
with woodcuts, 2 vols in
one, 8vo, *half morocco*,
t.e.g., uncut, 8s 6d [J.6] 1817

1065 **Vergil** (Polydore) English History, from an early translation, Vol. I., containing the first eight books, comprising the period prior to the Norman Conquest, edited by Sir Henry Ellis, sq. 8vo, 4s 6d [J.1]   1846

1066 **Viccars** (Joanne) Decapla in Psalmos, sive Commentarius ex decem Linguis MSS. et impressis Hebr. Arab., Syriac, Chald. Rabbin., Graec., Roman, Ital., Hispan.

1076 **Weekly Entertainer** (The); or Agreeable and Instructive Repository, containing a Collection of Se-

lect Pieces both in Prose and Verse; Curious Anecdotes, Instructive Tales and Ingenious Essays on different subjects, Vol 41–42, 2 vols in 1, 8vo, *old boards, calf back (two pp. torn)*, 12s 6d [G.16]
Sherborne, 1803

With Index to Vol. 41. Short accounts of Ancient English Sports, Balloons, Cockfighting, Origin of War, Rebellion in Ireland, etc.

1077 ——— Ditto, Vols 43–44, 2 vols in 1, 8vo, *old boards, calf back (no index)*, 10s [G.16]
Sherborne, 1804

Late Rebellion in Ireland (continued), Origin of April Fool's-day, Trial for Bigamy, Ceylon, St. Domingo, etc.

And below the wrapper:

be another habitable World in the Moon, with a Discourse concerning the possibility of a Passage thither. Unto which is added a Discourse concerning a new Planet, tending to prove that 'tis probable our Earth is one of the Planets, 8vo, *fourth edition, old calf, binding stained and wormed*, 7s 6d   1684

1083. **Zoology. — Moufet** (Thomas). Insectorum sive minimorum animalium theatrum. Fol. **First Edition.** *Old Calf, badly broken, titlepage missing*, £1 10s   1634

1084 ——— The Silkewormes, and their flies: lively described in verse, by T. M. a Countrie Farmer. 4to. **First Edition,** *rebound in calf. Pages stained*, £1 5s   1599

My dear Bishop Wilkins and my dear Dr. Moufet, looking up at me from parallel columns. It is apparent that I cannot waste-paper them without a look; I have the greatest regard for them both, the insectophile French physician, and the mathematical, ingenious, speculative Bishop of Chester, who so happily pursued his mechanical, astronomical and philosophical researches throughout wars and tumults, and got so prosperously, so discreetly, through the Civil War, Commonwealth, Protectorate, and Restoration, ending a Bishop and a member of the Royal Society; who, after the Restoration, "stood up for the Church of England, but dislik'd Vehemence in little and unnecessary Things, and freely censur'd it as Fanaticism on both sides"; for, in truth, his mind was up among the moon and planets, or speculating on how men might best fly, or thinking out levers, screws, wheels, pulleys and wedges. This book here will be, of course, *The Discovery of a New World in the Moon.*

The wrapper is slit and cast off. One may as well mark the *New World in the Moon;* no harm can come of marking it. And, now that the catalogue is opened, it would be foolish not to run an eye over the rest of it, just to see what is here. There may be another Bishop Wilkins.

There *is* another Bishop Wilkins—*Mathematicall Magick,* 1680 edition. How fortunate that I opened this catalogue, for I have been wanting a cheap *Mathematicall Magick* for months. And here is a modern reprint of John Maplet's *Greene Forest.* As I know of no other edition since the sixteenth century, I may as well mark it, though I remember its introduction to be foolish and sentimental, and of the "quaint old Maplet" type. Better is Burnet's *Sacred Theory of the Earth,* Third Edition, review'd by the Author, broken back and damaged boards, 1697. And William Shipway's

Campanalogia; or, Universal Instruction in the Art of Ringing, in Three Parts: to which is prefixed an Account of the Origin of Bells in Churches, with the Principal Peals in England, cr. 8vo, orig. boards, nice copy, uncut, 1816. Not that I need it: quite definitely, I do not need it at all; still, I will put a tick against it, in case I wish to refer to its title again.

1104. Yonge (C.M.) *Der Erbe von Redcliffe, aus dem Englischen* . . . Vol. I only, Author's Own Copy, 5s., Leipzig, 1856. Dear Heir of Redcliffe: I should like to see how your flashing eye and curling upper lip would go in German; but I will not; it would be desecration; *Der Erbe* shall have no tick.

Nor shall any of these modern first editions. Why does anyone prefer a first edition of a modern book to a later one? I am told that this is one of the diseases that one cannot hope to understand unless one suffers from it. It is, I presume, called protophilism, or even protomania. Sufferers from it keep, perhaps, the first white stone they see when out walking, or the newspapers for the first day of each month, or the top button off each of their coats, or the first stamp out of each stamp-book, or the programmes of the first nights of plays, or the firstlings of the infant year. Jehovah collected firstborns, alike of men, beasts, and plants, saying, "They are mine," so the instinct has high and ancient origin.

There are a number of firstlings in this catalogue. They are pathetically cheap. Ezra Pound, D. H. Lawrence, *John Halifax, Gentleman,* Jerome K. Jerome,

The Way of an Eagle, and a company of others, many of them "nice copies," and all about three shillings apiece. Does anyone buy them? I could, for my part, read lists of modern firsts for ever, and remain as full in purse as when I began; I never feel "they are mine." I could wish that catalogues contained nothing else, and were not, instead, alive with more perilous seductions.

How these lure one down the page! We are arrived at the P's; PEZRON (M.) *The Antiquities of Nations; English by Mr. Jones,* 8vo. calf, stained, 1706. PLAYS. Samuel Foote, calf gilt, cracked, label missing, 8s 6d, 1799. PLINY. *Naturall Historie of C. Plinius Secundus. Trans. by Philemon Holland, very worn.* . . . POL-WHELE (R.) *The Influence of Local Attachment with respect to Home,* joint cracked, 4s 6d. POPISH CRUELTY EXEMPLIFIED *in the various Sufferings of Mr. Serres & several other French Gentlemen, done into English by Claud D'Assas,* calf, a few leaves stained, 5s 6d, 1723. . . .

And so down to Zola and Zoology, the former of which seems to remain a bore, even in a catalogue, while the latter is so enticing that to read the names of its dryest manuals is a stimulant.

A stimulant: yes, the word is apt. To read these catalogues is like drinking wine in the middle of the morning; it elevates one into that state of felicitous intoxication in which one feels capable of anything. I must control myself, and not write to booksellers in haste: there must be a gap between the perusal of the catalogue and my postcard. Drinking, said Dr. Johnson, should be practised with great prudence; one must have skill in inebriation. A man without such skill will undertake anything. . . . I will wait until the effects are worn off, and then write a postcard sober, temperate, moderate, brief, restrained. . . .

But, while I wait, those more intemperate than myself will have rushed in and bought *Mathematicall Magick*, the *New World in the Moon*, the *Theatre of Insects*, and the *Silkewormes*. It is obvious that I cannot wait. Probably I should telephone. . . .

I need a new bookshelf. I am short of money. I could have read all these books in the British Museum; some of them even from the London Library. In short, I am sober again. But I am glad that I was drunk.

BULLS

BULLS

How agreeable to watch, from the other side of the high stile, this mighty creature, this fat bull of Bashan, snorting, champing, pawing the earth, lashing the tail, breathing defiance at heaven and at me, crooning in ignoble rage (for rage is always ignoble when both causeless and ill-directed). How mighty are his sinews, how stout and fierce his horns, how fiery his nostrils, how strong and huge his thews! Did he that made the lamb make him? He is a very king of cows. One sees him roaming the great prairies, lord of a herd, rounded up by cowboys with cracking whips.

> *That lordly Bull of mine. . . .*
> *How loudly to the hills he croons,*
> *That croon to him again!*

And now here he stands, so near and yet so far, his heart hot with hate, unable to climb a stile.

But suppose that, using his horns as battering-rams, he should rush at it and break it down?

CANDLEMAS

CANDLEMAS

THE parroco came before each Candlemas Day to
bless the house. He would walk about it, sprinkling
holy water, and he would bring each year a tall and
lovely candle of entwined and multi-coloured wax,
which he had blessed. We had, too, a number of little
candles, made of long spirals of coloured wax twisted
close and coiled up like a snake, to be uncoiled as they
burned down. They were red and green and yellow
and blue, and of great beauty. We took them out
with us for our Candlemas picnic, which consisted
of oranges, a few preserved fruits, dates and prunes,
and fragments of rolls. This feast we took with us
along the Savona or the Genoa road, or along the river,
or up the hill path behind the house, that climbed,
stony and steep, past the carob-tree to our rock houses.
Arrived at these craggy piles and promontories, we
sat down, lit our coloured candles, and stood them
on stones. Rearing slim necks to heaven, they burned,
frail and flickering golden buds, while we gnawed
bread, sucked oranges, kept the exquisiteness of preserved fruits and French plums for the last *bonne
bouche*, and, having finished all, but being still loth
to cease, plucked myrtle berries and so prolonged the
feast. Some of these were black and plump, almost

sweet, others immature and sharp. At any stage, they were better than juniper berries, which dried the mouth.

Thus we kept Candlemas, looking over a wide blue bay through a pink shimmer of almond blossom, while the town below made festa, and a procession wound, harshly chanting, through the deep and narrow streets to Santa Caterina's pink church at the hill's foot. In the still and resinous air our candle-flames burned like little tulips, the flower elongating as the stem dwindled. Thrifty, we would not unwind all the coils and burn them out. The feast done, we extinguished the tapers and put them by for future use. The Candlemas festa thus kept with pious rites, the rock houses became castles to be besieged.

But we had an annual Candlemas difference of opinion with our father, for we thought Candlemas should be a holiday from lessons. Not so he; and he won. So Candlemas Day was wasted until the afternoon.

CANOEING

CANOEING

A GREAT curve of smooth blue Mediterranean spreads between my frail bark and the distant line of shore. I slip down an azure orange, a swelling and limpid mountainside; I perceive about me what one has always heard, that the earth is indeed a ball. I can still just, when I turn my head and look, spy the bay, the shore, the town, the church towers, the house on the shore to the bay's east, nestling beneath and in front of a jagged line of piney, terraced hills and of the wild running steeps of higher Apennines behind these. But a few minutes, a few strokes of the paddle, and all but the hills will be sunk, vanished, drowned below the rim of the round world.

I turn again and look: the town, the shore, are gone; I am alone with a blue horizon ahead (beyond lies Corsica, but I shall not see that island), the mountain rim of the bay behind, a long jut of soft indigo grey (Savona) thrusting out into western sea and sky, the further and fainter blue point of Genoa lying twenty miles east, bounding the great bay, and beyond that Spezia, pale and shimmering as fairyland, for there, so one has been told, are marble mountains.

On the ocean's rim flies a far ship with spread sails, like a gull. I am alone; I navigate uncharted seas, where the known stars are laid asleep in Tethys' lap; where neither birds can instruct to any near shore, nor any birds in the main Ocean to be seen; where without the compass all things are out of compass, and nothing but miracle or chance can save or serve. I am of the great company of hazardous mariners who brave the deep; I am Captain Cook, Columbus, Cabot, Magellan, Raleigh, Drake; I am Jack, Ralph and Peterkin exploring round their Coral Island; I am an officer of the Royal Navy, sent out on a lone mission to spy out slavers, pirates, French or Spanish men-of-war; or I seek treasure left absent-mindedly on a small island long since, and the secret chart, yellow with age, without which I can never arrive there, lies folded against my breast.

I am the first that ever burst into this silent sea. Perils beleaguer me on every side. There a sharp fin pierces the smooth surface like a sail; a white belly gleams as a giant shark turns on its back. He rushes on me through the deep, with open jaws: one lurch of his body beneath my canoe, and it and I would be hurled out of the water, and down again into that ravening mouth. Only one thing to do—the trick learned of the Coral Islanders: I wait until the monster is close, wait until he turns on his back, then, with a mighty thrust, insert the end of the paddle between his jaws. He threshes about in the water; the canoe is swirled round, as I cling fast to the paddle: but before long he chokes and sinks down into the deep, a corpse, fortunately spewing forth the paddle before doing so. I am saved; but I believe that his widow and little ones, his infuriate and formidable bereaved (sharks being very family fish), are not far distant, and may at any moment apprehend the situation and give chase. It behoves me to be wary.

Also, that sail on the horizon is, beyond doubt, a pirate sail: if it should sight me, I am lost. And at any moment I might be surrounded by canoes fraught with savages. There are mermaids too, and mermen, leaping and diving, shooting up from the bottom of the monstrous world to spy and peer at the gallant young sailor in his frail bark. To entertain me, they strike their harps with a most melodious twang, and sing sea chanties. Here too are flying-fish, and there is that leviathan; he even spouts; every marvel of the perilous deep displays itself before the explorer's sophisticated and unastonished eyes.

Of a sudden the deep heaves and swells; the canoe lurches up and down. I am dismayed and astonished, I reel to and from like a drunken man. For a ship bears towards me; a real ship, a steamer in full tilt, rushing towards Genoa; in her wake the white foam flies, the furrow follows free; she disturbs the ocean with her passing, and like a cockle-shell my bark rocks. Peril assumes the sterner face of reality; pirates, mermaids, and sharks vanish into blue sea and air; I toss alone in a canoe on the heaving main; she may overturn. Often enough she overturns nearer shore, when the waves run high or the crew are restless; that makes no matter, for we sit on her bottom and navigate her upside down. But to overturn alone, far out on the round sea's curve, out of sight, out of swimming distance, of land; perhaps to sink—that is another matter. As to sharks, they exist; one was thrown up on the beach near Cogoleto lately; a man bathing off Albissola was once killed. . . . Sharks are real, and the canoe is lurching up hills, valing down valleys, bobbing and leaping like a porpoise or a cork.

The ship passes on her way; the heaving sea's long roll lessens, little and little, until the blue level which is really a curve spreads again from east to west, from north to south.

But fear has looked in, chill phantom among golden dreams. I no more desire to paddle south into the boundless main, into the Ligurian sea towards Corsica, for ever sliding down the curving world, further with every stroke of the paddle from my home bay. I paddle shoreward quickly, as if a shoal of monsters of the deep gave chase; I climb the blue glass ball again, slipping higher and higher up its limpid side, until below the hills the coast road appears, and the little many-coloured town, curved around its bay, arises like a drowned city, a lost Atlantis from which an ocean drops, exposing it once more to view. Detail appears: churches, pink or yellow or striped black and white; the stone archways that lead from town to shore; palms, oranges, lemons, eucalyptus, luxuriantly topping garden walls and burgeoning on terraces ("from whence," as Mr. John Evelyn, coasting the Riviera, wrote, "might perfectly be smelt the peculiar joys of Italy in the perfumes of orange, citron, and jassmine flowers, for divers leagues seaward"). And now I can perceive the fishing-boats and nets lying on the sands; and the square red house beyond the town, with the slope of beach running down from its garden to the sea's edge.

Land; safety; port for the sailor home from the sea; the end of an adventure. The angelus ringing across the bay; hens clucking; the lisping and hissing of tiny waves on sand; the late afternoon soaking hills and shore with golden heat. Gliding in to shore with the ripples, stepping out into warm, knee-deep water, dragging the canoe until she rests on dry beach. Voices that plain like gulls—"It's not fair, taking her out alone and keeping her out all that time. We're going a voyage to the rocks. . . ."

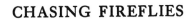

CHASING FIREFLIES

CHASING FIREFLIES

EACH midsummer eve, after dark, we would go a fire-fly walk. The way started through a little orto, where a vine trellis arched over a shadowed path, and orange-and lemon-trees bordered it, standing against white walls and filling the velvet night with sweetness, as the frogs in every little reservoir and ditch filled it with melody. Beyond the orto, the path climbed up between terraces, where the olive trees cast delicate black shadows on the moonlit stairway, and orange and lemon groves still perfumed the night. Among them, and all about the myrtle shrubs and juniper and little pines, capered and leaped the fireflies, flying between the cold moon and the earth. They pranced and danced, they twinked and blinked, they sparked, they larked, they burned like flying stars, like leap-ing gems, and after them we sped beneath a huge golden moon, scrambling up rocks, jumping down terraces, plunging scratched hands into juniper bushes, standing still against sticky pine-trunks to tempt the brilliant creatures near. Too rarely our cupped hands closed on a spark and held it, while it blinked at us shyly, on and off, like a lighthouse. Not to all was it given to catch a firefly; it was an event, a triumph; to hold one was to hold a magicking imp, that now burnt like a star, now darkly brooded, a sullen insect without joy.

"If you find any pretty insects, keep them in a box," Dr. Browne of Norwich wrote to his son in France. So also did we desire to do. But authority was against us; we were given to understand that in boxes our fireflies would pine, extinguish, and die. So we released the lucent sparks; they fled to join the host of dancing candles that bespangled the hills.

In the midsummer moonlight, with enormous golden stars empatining a violet sky, and these tiny bright ones skipping among black shadows about the lemon-sweet, frog-sung mountains, the world on St. John's Eve was incredible yet familiar, like worlds known in dreams.

But they never would let us stay out in it all night.

CHRISTMAS MORNING

CHRISTMAS MORNING

CHRISTMAS woke me early, in the small dark hours, as
if someone had touched me on the shoulder and said,
Wake up, wake up, it's Christmas. I woke up and it
was dark, and would not be Christmas for hours. I
crawled to the foot of the bed, to where it hung on
the painted iron bedrail, the large woollen stocking
that had yawned so emptily overnight, but now so
stiffly, bulkily, swollenly bulged. It might not be
opened until daylight, but I felt it outside, pinching
and poking its various protuberances, from the square
cornery one above the knee to the round one in the toe
that might be an orange or a glass witchball. Shivers
of ecstasy curdled my blood as I fingered and felt; my
hair stared, my skin goosed, my pulses hammered in
heart and head. It was Christmas Day. However often
I whispered it, I could scarcely credit so strange, so
preposterous, so heavenly a fact. Christmas Day had
indeed arrived. But how could it really, actually, in
point of fact, have come, and I in bed as usual, in
the same red flannel pyjamas as on any other night?
Yet Christmas Day must come; one had long expected
it, and here it was. Perhaps it was a dream.

But of a sudden the still dark was shaken and shattered and a-clamour with bells. Not the gay sweet

chiming of an English church peal, but harsh, clanging, iron, tremendous, a very roar and tumult of noise. The great Roman brick tower of Sant Ambrogio in the large piazza outside the windows, the striped black and white tower of San Domenico in the small piazza up the street, the more distant, but patronal, Santa Caterina along the sea road beyond the town, the church of the Collegio up the hill path, the chapel of the convent school, all with one accord awoke to Christmas morning and clanged their summons to Mass. They were insistent, commanding, almost menacing. English bells, sweetly and uncertainly tumbling as they chime, seem to sing, *Come along to church, good people if you please, come along to church on Christmas Day*. These bells cry, *Venite, venite, il Signore v'aspetta, levatevi pronto, pronto, e fate il dovere*.

But to me they only shouted, *Christmas Day! Christmas Day!*

Soon the piazza and streets were alive with hurrying feet, and with such resonant cries as Italians emit even between bed and Mass.

I crawled back under the bed-clothes and curled up to wait for Christmas Day. When it should be held to have fully arrived, we should all assemble on one bed and open the stockings. To me, lying in the clanging dark, forbidden to go and wake others before it was light, the propitious and blest day seemed half the night away. How foolishly the others slept, oblivious of the jubilant occasion!

   Full little thought they than
   That the mighty Pan
   Was kindly come to live with them below;
 Perhaps their loves, or els their sheep,
 Was all that did their silly thoughts so busie keep.

Whatever it was, and regardless of the bells, they slept like pigs in straw.

CHURCH-GOING

CHURCH-GOING

1. *Anglican*

How dignified, how stately, how elegant, with ranks of tapers wavering gold against a dim background, while boys' voices lift the psalm *Audite hæc, omnes* high above the pealing organ to the high embowed roof, to linger and wander there among ten thousand cells. Through the windows richly dight, slant crimson, violet and deep blue rays of October evening sunshine; it touches the round heads and white surplices of little singing boys; it glints on the altar, dimming the tall, flickering flames, gleaming on the heads of thoughtful clergymen who listen to the quire's chant. *For he shall carry nothing away with him when he dieth: neither shall his pomp follow him. For while he lived he counted himself an happy man: and so long as thou doest well unto thyself, men will speak good of thee. He shall follow the generation of his fathers: and shall never see light. Man being in honour hath no understanding: but is compared unto the beasts that perish. . . .*

The soft and melancholy chant dies on a falling lilt. The clergy, quire and people sit down in deep oak seats, all but the lector, who rustles to the lectern, adjusts his pince-nez, and says gently, "*Here begin-neth the first verse of the sixth chapter of the Book of Micah. Hear ye now what the Lord saith: Arise, contend thou before the mountains, and let the hills hear thy voice. . . .*"

The musical Eton-and-Cambridge monotone, just not parsonically pitched, strolls on, relating the Lord's controversy in the mountains with his people. I turn the pages of my Prayer Book, read the charming rubrics, read the Preface, of 1662, so gentlemanlike, so suavely urbane. *It hath been the wisdom of the Church of England, ever since the first compiling of her Publick Liturgy, to keep the mean between the two extremes. . . .*

And then, Of Ceremonies, why some be abolished and some retained. . . . *And moreover, they be neither dark nor dumb ceremonies, but are so set forth, that every man may understand what they do mean, and to what use they do serve. . . . And in these our doings we condemn no other Nations, nor prescribe anything but to our own people only: For we think it con-venient that every Country should use such Cere-monies as they shall think best to the setting forth of God's honour and glory, and to the reducing of the people to a most perfect and godly living. . . .*

Meanwhile, the Eton-and-Cambridge voice is gently putting searching inquiries, becoming reluctantly men-acing. *Are there yet*, it asks, *the treasures of wicked-ness in the house of the wicked, and the scant measure that is abominable? Shall I count them pure with the wicked balances, and with the bag of deceitful weights? . . . Therefore also will I make thee sick in smiting thee, in making thee desolate because of thy sins. Thou shalt eat, but not be satisfied. . . . Thou shalt sow, but thou shalt not reap; thou shalt tread the olives, but thou shalt not anoint thee with oil, and sweet wine, but shalt not drink wine. . . . That I should make thee a desolation, and the inhabitants thereof a hissing. . . .*

It has grown too violent, this mountain controversy. *Here endeth the first Lesson,* and so to the Magnificat. One feels that it was time.

These violent Hebrews: they break in strangely, with hot Eastern declamation and gesture, into our tranquil Anglican service, our so ordered and so decent Common Prayer. A desolation and a hissing: those are not threats that our kindly clergy like to quote, even against those of their flock who have abominable scant measures and wicked balances. Milton railed against "the oppressions of a simonious, decimating clergy," but, though they cannot help (since they must live) being decimating, they are no longer so simonious, and are a kindly race.

As to these services, which they long since so gracefully adapted, so fitly, beautifully, and ceremoniously translated and assembled, they are, as Sir John Suckling pointed out three centuries ago, fit for the attendance of even the fastidious Cato, who was disgusted by those of his own age and country. "Then," complained the shocked Sir John, "the Ceremonies of

Liber Pater and *Ceres*, how obscene! and those Days
which were set apart for the Honour of the Gods,
celebrated with such shews as *Cato* himself was
ashamed to be present at. On the contrary, our Services are such, as not only *Cato*, but God himself may
be there."

Or so, at least, we hope. No doubt the Romans
hoped too that Liber Pater and Ceres were present
with them at worship, and that their lectisternia were
enjoyed by the reclining and feasting deities. Be that as
it may, and whatever the gods may think of it (and
one must endeavour not to fall into arrogance in this
matter of divine attendance at our worship), for my
part I greatly admire and enjoy the Anglican order.

Though of course there is, from time to time, a
sermon. . . . But it seems that this cannot, in any
Church, be helped.

2. *Roman Catholic*

Is it because they happen to be the earliest in my
memory, that the churches in a small Italian fishing-
town still seem to me to be the very concentrated es-
sence of what we mean when we say "church"? Or
is it one's mediæval heritage, from the centuries that
stretch back through time, through ages of mystery,
of what our civilised Anglican Prayer Book calls dark
and dumb ceremonies, of harsh chanting in dog-Latin,
of swinging censers that smother the musty air and
human odours with drifting clouds of aromatic sweet-

ness? From whatever cause, when I think "church," I am back in a great, cool, dim, pillared interior, shut from a sunlit piazza by heavy leather door-curtains, clouded with drifts of that agreeable smoke which, while it ascends to heaven, fortunately perfumes all about it, and which we have always so rightly and wisely offered to our gods. Indeed, those churches which do not do so probably make a tactical error which no audible or visual beauty can redeem. Amid these fragrant clouds we advance, past the stoup of holy water which, thinks my mother, needs more frequent changing than it gets, past the notice on the wall which pleads, alas how vainly, "Per l'onore di Dio, e per l'igiene, si prega di non sputare," into the dim interior, full of scraping wooden chairs, standing men, and old women kneeling as they mutter over their beads. One of these interrupts her orisons to put out a gnarled brown hand to my mother, murmuring mechanically "*Ave Maria, piena di grazia*, un soldino, signora, per l'amore di Dio. *Santa Maria, Madre di Dio, prega per noi peccatori, adesso e nell' ora della nostra morte.*" We kneel on chairs, our chins resting on their backs, and listen to that nasally monotonous chanting which seems to be the most widely and long approved tone in which to address one's God. Anyhow to me it seemed, and seems, to have a certain fitness and rightness which less primitive accents lack. It seems the voice of the whole world at worship; a black savage, an Australian aborigine, would surely feel at home with it, as with the fragrant smoking spices and gums, and the gaudily clad wax or plaster figures who stand in niches round the church, some cruelly transfixed with swords or arrows, some enwreathed with paper flowers, but all with patient eyes upturned to heaven, and all with rows of candles guttering about them. A charming hagiary; I could not then, I cannot now, hear them scorned without resentment. Often one or another of them would be carried by a procession, on his or her festa, out of church and all round the town, and then they appeared to greater advantage than ever. Those adorable processions: I can scarcely admit to the status of a real religion a church which does not have them. A church, like a monarchy, must be potentially and occasionally processional, must show itself for worship and jubilee in the open, must at times be peregrinating and agoral, and wind, rich in pomps and gauds, through marketplace, street and town. Pomps and gauds, chanting and sweet smells, ceremonious adoration and mystery—if these be not the fit circumstance and habit of worship, the worshipping world has for many thousands of years erred.

At all events, when I say "church," I am incenseshrouded, wax-saint-surrounded, kneeling on a highbacked chair on an uneven stone floor much *sputato*, among neighbours who tell their beads and have eaten garlic, and the primitive, eternal chanting drones on before a gaudy high altar, where peasant priests, richly vestured, genuflect, advance and retreat in stately measure. From the sun-baked piazza without come the voices of men, who, in order not to waste their time, are waiting for the essential moment to enter, and meanwhile are lounging outside the drogheria, or hitting a ball through hoops. And, through and beyond this male clatter, there whispers, sighs and lisps the delicately turning edge of the summer sea, running lightly up the sand, drawing back, rustling like a cicada's wings.

But see, one of the priests is in the pulpit; he is preaching about *l'inferno*, its horrid and enduring torments. Well, that too is primitive; one hears in it the rolling thunders of the Christian Church down the ages, the awful fulminations, denunciations, miniations, of saints, popes, councils, prophets and poets, who have never scrupled or boggled at fiery damnation, or at the horrid picture of Satan and his tailed minions at work. Like pomp and ceremony, hell also has always been part of religion. Anglicans have forgotten it, have gently, rationally and fastidiously damped down and blurred over that fiery scarlet patch in the cosmography of religion, turning it into a vague cloud which they call the unsearchable and incalculable mercy of God. You will hear no hell-fire sermons from them; and when one of the creeds formulated by Councils in less delicate ages speaks with zest of without doubt perishing everlastingly, there is an Anglican agitation to have it omitted from services.

But there is no such squeamish humanitarian nonsense about Roman Catholics, and to this day you may hear from Irish and Latin pulpits the genuine old-world sizzling of frying souls, which gives such zest to being still above ground, such determination to make a good end.

The sermon is over; the preacher descends; for a moment one hears again that rustling, sighing whisper from the seashore, before the chant of Christian believers sings above it: *Credo in unum Deum, Patrem omnipotentem, factorem coeli et terræ visibilium omnium et invisibilium. . . .*

3. *Quaker*

The seventeenth century meeting-house stands in a dell in a beech-wood; it is built of mellowed, lichened brick, with latticed windows and whitewashed walls and a gallery running round. Outside the clear glass windows green beech waves, and dark green holly sharply twinkles. The door stands open, and through it sounds the singing of birds, the call of a cuckoo, and the running, leaping and chattering of squirrels. The Friends sit in stillness, waiting on the Spirit, who will presently move some one to rise and speak. For my part, I shall not be ill-pleased should the Spirit move no one this morning, except the squirrels and the birds and that distant hen who would appear to have produced an egg.

But the Spirit is, as usual, stirring. The caretaker of the meeting-house gets up; he speaks about the happy birds, mentioning also the more agreeable among the insects, such as butterflies, who, says he, are also happy. He refers to the cuckoo, who so soon must fly, with that intelligence bestowed on him so amply by the Lord and so profitably used throughout his English trip, to warmer lands. Happiness: taking no care: this appears, perhaps naturally, to be the caretaker's ambition; his view is that happiness is widely experienced among the feathered and the winged, and that the reason for this is that they take no care, but trust in the Lord. He even appears to be interpreting the piping parliament among the trees as a meeting for worship. Can he be right? And do birds believe, and tell one another, that human beings are happy? And do we perhaps exaggerate the carefreedom of our plumy fellow-creatures, who obviously have their troubles, some of them more troublesome than those which normally visit man? Squirrels, for example. . . . Still, it gives pleasure to the caretaker, a generous and unenvious man, to think that birds are happy and take no care.

He resumes his seat, having left with us these interesting speculations, over which we meditate for a while, until the Spirit moves again. This time we have a little talk about the importance of making our wills, lest we be cut off intestate, thus causing trouble and confusion among our survivors. The speaker must, I think, be a solicitor. He speaks well: we make mental notes: *Will: make it at once.* He is a more practical man than the caretaker. The caretaker cannot, surely, much approve his advice, for his own was to live like the birds, looking not ahead, but trusting that the

Lord would arrange. The birds do not make wills. That is one of the points about Meeting—you get all points of view. The next is that of a kind-faced woman, who has been sitting surrounded by children, whom she has been successfully pacifying and rendering innocuous for half an hour and has now led out and set free. Returning to her place, she speaks about children. One wonders again, why do children, so attractive in life, become in discourse so uninteresting? Perhaps people say the wrong things about them. . . . They become, on the tongue of this kind woman, strangely like the birds of the caretaker—happy, care-free, trusting, very religious. In another moment, one feels, she will be saying that those cheerful voices receding through the woods are raised in the praise of God. But no; she does not go so far as that. She is either a mother or a school teacher, and knows children better than the caretaker knows birds. Still, the children of her discourse are shadowy little cherubs, simple-minded, almost winged; by no means the stormy, questioning, imagination-haunted, earthy, ingenious, gluttonous, perverse, exciting and excited little creatures that we know. Those who thus think of children set one wondering at what point the Great Change occurs which turns them into the so different adults that they become. The children they envisage would have been approved by Pelagius, for they have no original sin; they seem ready to die straight away, like a child by Charles Dickens, and wing their way to heaven.

After this, a speaker is moved to talk of living by

conscience. He is practical, idealistic, spiritual, ethical, stirring. He makes it seem, while he speaks, almost possible that humanity should live in such a strange, unusual manner. He brings righteousness into the foreground. . . . Is this where most churches fail? If they would give religion a rest and concentrate on ethics, who knows what odd results might follow? When the Friends, as they frequently do, speak thus, one understands the disturbing and unwelcome emotions of dislike that they used, in less tolerant centuries, to arouse, so that all the warring churches, Anglican, Roman Catholic, Presbyterian, Anabaptist, and the rest, were united when they saw, heard of, or thought of Quakers, by a common and fervent desire to whip them, to set them in stocks, to brand them with hot irons, to fling them into dark cells for life.

How many a meeting, in this very house, has been held in the shadow of these fearful intentions! They seem still to lurk in the beech woods, to be creeping along the deep lane, the constable with his posse of men coming to catch the Quakers red-handed at their damned conventicling blasphemy, to arrest them and hale them off in chains to the magistrate, there to be sentenced to the whip, the stocks and the gaol. The rustling squirrels, the leaping rabbits in the undergrowth, they are the steps of spies, the tramping of armed men, coming to seize us in the name of the King, the Church, and the Laws.

Still, if we live according to the implanted light of conscience . . . that is what the quiet-voiced speaker is saying. . . . Even in gaol and the stocks we could, we suppose, do that—if indeed we could ever do such an extraordinary thing. . . . But, anyhow, what an idea! Much better sing psalms, hymns, anthems, swing censers, praise the Lord. It is time that I slipped out of this meeting, into the woods.

4. *Unitarian*

It is certainly ugly, with its varnished deal seats and green paint. What a pity that those who believe on the Trinity have secured all the best churches! Still, there must be some temporal penalty for those who cannot thus think; not so long since, they used to burn them, and we know, from the Athanasian creed, in what predicament they will find themselves after death. Green painted hot water pipes and varnished yellow deal are, doubtless, their punishment in this life for gainsaying that long line of theologians who have, with no uncertain voice, instructed them through nineteen centuries on the tremendous Triune Mystery. Similar, indeed, is the punishment, in this country, of most of the dissenters from Ecclesia Anglicana, who seldom seem to be able to build good churches for themselves. (Westminster Cathedral is a notable exception.) Anyhow, this Unitarian chapel is a sad ugly place, and must pain its thoughtful, earnest, attentive worshippers and the pale, eager young minister who is preaching about the barren fig-tree. He is concerned about this fig-tree; the story of how it was cursed and sterilised for evermore troubles him; he cannot see that it was a right way to behave to an innocent tree; perhaps he has a fig-tree of his own at home. That Trinitarians should have related and believed such a story down the ages throws for him an unfortunate light on the mentality of Trinitarians down the ages.

But this was, for him, not necessary. He, and we, already knew that Trinitarians down the ages have been like that. We have found our way to a purer, a more tolerant, a more rational faith. The pleasure of enjoying this, of being so rational, so tolerant, and so pure, lifts our hearts and swells our voices as we sing our monotheistic hymns, from which all references to the Holy Ghost have been expunged. In our kindly voices rings that superiority which comes from never having burnt Trinitarians, Tritheists, or atheists, nor whipped Quakers; no, nor wished to. The first Arians may, it is true, have committed a few excesses against Athanasians, but that was merely because they got out of hand in a hot climate. Since then, all has been with us sweet reasonableness, kindness and light. Photinians, Macedonians, Sabellians, Socinians, Ebionites, Dr. Martineau, all our so rational predecessors hover around us, a small but intelligent cloud of witnesses, delighted that their heresy, so long abhorred, persecuted, despised, is at length permitted to express itself freely in a green and yellow chapel smelling of hot water pipes.

There was a period in my youthful career when I used to think, if one could believe at all, it would be in the Unitarian God. It seemed so easy, so comparatively reasonable. . . . But, alas, the Unitarians undid themselves with me by their architectural and ritual inadequacies. Nevertheless, there is a very pure and intelligent atmosphere about their worship, and they are very right to see through the fig-tree story.

CINEMA

CINEMA

NEVER a dull moment! From a bright foyer we descend in darkness down a slope lit by the flashing torches of fantastic elves, dancing ahead like wills-o'-the-wisp until they settle, pointing us to seats in the middle of an eagerly gazing row of persons, past whom we push, to subside into plush chairs and eagerly gaze too. There is a news reel on; ships are being launched, royalties visit cities and are met by mayors; football is played in the rain before vast crowds, tennis flashes by like lightning, and is repeated in slow motion, horses race and leap, troops walk past with that jerky gait peculiar to animated photography, Signor Mussolini, roaring wide-mouthed like a bull of Bashan, harangues the people of Italy; all is bustle and energy. One feels that ours is a busy world, wherein humanity scuttles about like ants, each bearing his little burden. It is not very like the world which we see about us; still, it is a little too like to be really good entertainment, and we are pleased when it abruptly ceases and the screen burgeons into the colour and fantastic nonsense of a Silly Symphony. This is what films ought to show us; they should assist in the process of apotheosising the absurd. This is, indeed, what they do throughout, even when they mimic life, and this is why I prefer them to flesh and blood miming on the stage, which is often so near life as to be tedious. This flat, two-dimensioned moving photography can never be at all like life; it is the most charming, the most bizarre, the most ludicrous convention. See how flowers ring bells and sing, how trees turn into forest demons, how hares play lawn tennis, leaping over the net to take the ball they have served! And, the Silly Symphony over, the Big Picture begun, how the photographs representing persons run about, emitting, in metallic, hollow voices and the lilt of the Californian tongue, the most improbable remarks. Those young British officers, trained at Sandhurst and pursuing their vocation on the Indian frontier, have obviously profited by a career of film-seeing, for they speak the purest Hollywood. So does the little Scottish minister, which is stranger, for he lived before films were. So too does that Roman Empress, and the proud patrician Marcus, but that is all right; if you translate the speech of foreigners, it may as well be into American as into English. The remarkable thing is that any of these photographs should speak at all. It is like women preaching, or dogs walking on their hind legs.

See how that daring young man leaps from his aeroplane in mid air, sailing in his parachute so as to alight on the roof of the house in Chinatown where the gangsters have the girl tied up. Can you beat it? Certainly not on the stage; probably not in life. That is the beauty of the films; they expand life, puff it up into a ludicrous, incredible, magnificent balloon, set it soar-

ing through space, cut loose from the ropes which tie
it down to fact. Then, how well they photograph raging seas, glaciers, deserts, mountain peaks, penguins,
grasshoppers, and wild beasts prowling through jungles.
Battles, too; here are Waterloo and Plassey in little,
terrible with battling elephants and upping Guards.
Had Shakespeare known of such a way of miming
Agincourt, how he would have rejoiced! And in what
unearthly, horrid and transparent shapes would his
ghosts have revisited the glimpses of the moon, in
place of the too solid flesh in which perforce dead
Cæsar and King Hamlet stalked the boards and stalk
them to this day. As to his fairies, in what elegant and
dainty minuteness would Titania and Oberon meet and
square, while their elves for fear crept into acorn cups
and hid them there.

There is, to be sure, one thing that moving photography should never attempt; that is to portray serious
and actual human drama, the relations between human
creatures. Indeed, why should they? These we can see
all about us in life, and very weary of them we get.
To be confronted with them again on the screen would
be too much. Indeed, I seldom am so, since I choose
my films with care. They should be funny, fantastic,
exotic, anything they like, but not human. Love they
should shun like the devil; it is not for photographs,
however animated, nor for mechanically recorded
voices, however Hollywood, to mime this universal
terrestrial passion. Let the films know their business,
and lead us tip-toe through strange fantastic realms,

soaring above the clouds, burrowing in the bowels of the earth, galloping across cactus deserts among mesquite and Gila monsters, pursued by Sheriffs, zigzagging in wild and rickety cars pursued by the constabulary, grappling with monsters of the deep or of the trackless jungle, wooing humour with the suave voice and face of Mr. Laughton, the impassivity of Mr. Harold Lloyd, the rolling eyes of Mr. Cantor, improbable legs and the impossible figure of Mr. Jack Hulbert and Miss Courtneidge, the imbecility of Mr. Ralph Lynn, the glitter of Miss Lyn Fontaine. Once they stoop, or attempt to stoop, to realism, they are undone, these wonderful contrivances. Heavens above, is there not enough realism in life, that our moving photographs should ape it?

Come away: a gripping drama has begun. Out, past still eagerly gazing rows; out into the night. If we must have gripping dramas, we prefer to see them in the world at large, where, alas, they are all too common. Our comic fairyland falls shattered about us at so crude a trumpet blast. We will adjourn to the Café Royal and consume sandwiches and bock.

CLOTHES

CLOTHES

How handsome it looks, my new dress, fresh from its maker's hands! How elegant, how eximious, how smug, how quaintly fashioned, how all that there is of the most modish! How like other people I shall appear when I wear it! With what respect they will regard me, saying one to another, Look, do you see that woman? She knows how to dress; she is in the mode; indeed, she looks very well. I think I have at other times seen her in dresses three, four, even five years old, altered, as she believes, but not really, to the discerning eye, altered to matter, for they still remain of their epoch, and insufferable to people of good taste and modern outlook, now that there is such gaudy going and such new fashions every day. But to-day she really has a new dress, and a good dress; to-day she really is a Well-Dressed Woman. I like its cut, do not you? And the colour is precisely right.

This is how (I trust) they will speak to one another of me and of my new dress, when they see it. How I shall prank it among them, "loitering up and down, peacocking and courting of myself." I shall feel as Adam felt when Eve made him (after, of course, their great and disastrous removal) a medley coat of feathers.

Eve, *walking forth about the Forrests, gathers*
Speights, Parrots, Peacocks, Estrich *scatt'red feathers*
And then with wax the smaller plumes she sears,
And sows the greater with long white Horse hairs . . .
And therof makes a medly coat so rare
That it resembles Nature's *Mantle faire,*
When in the Sun, in Pomp all glistering,
She seems with smiles to woo the gawdy Spring . . .

Then on he puts his painted garments new,
And Peacocke-like himselfe doth often view,
Looks on his shadow, and in proud amaze
Admires the hand that had the Art to cause
So many severall parts to meet in one,
To fashion thus the quainte Mandilion.

I shall feel as the serpent must feel in her new skin,
as the barrel-organ monkey in his new red jacket and
cocked hat. Strange, what a singular effect the body's
outer wrapping has on the mind, how it elevates or
depresses the termless spirit of man, exalting it to preen
its feathers among the plumy angels, abasing it to creep
the earth with meanest worm.

Foolish questions have been asked about this matter
by philosophers and moralists since human beings
began to put foolish questions at all. Dr. Watts, for
example, inquired.

> *Why should our garments, made to hide*
> *Our parents' shame, provoke our pride?*

*The art of dress did ne'er begin
Till Eve our mother learn'd to sin.*

*When first she put her covering on,
Her robe of innocence was gone;
And yet her children vainly boast
In the sad marks of glory lost.*

*How proud we are! how fond to shew
Our clothes, and call them rich and new!
When the poor sheep and silkworm wore
That very clothing long before.*

*The tulip and the butterfly
Appear in gayer coats than I;
Let me be drest fine as I will,
Flies, worms, and flowers, exceed me still.*

And, "Have you," Crœsus, adorned in his pomp and glory, inquired of Solon, "ever seen a goodlier spectacle?" "Yes," said Solon, "cocks, pheasants and peacocks."

Why, in short, the philosophers and moralists desire to know, should we that are earth, ashes and dust prick up ourselves so peacockly? They are but seldom answered, since the earth, ashes and dust is too busy pricking up itself to pause to reply to foolish questions. But the answer is apparent. Why does the crow emplume itself with gaudy borrowed quills? We that are so mean and plain cannot face our fellows without extraneous decking. Were we modelled out of crystal, jade and turquoise, of the lucent milky moonstone and the orient pearl, were we even fashioned like the small birds and pretty beasts, no adornment should we need or use. But nature has not thus privileged man. "If" (as Montaigne remarks) "we impartially enter into judgment with our selves, we shall find, that if there be any creature or beast less favoured in that than we, there are others (and that in greater numbers) to whom nature hath been more favourable than to us. *A multibus animalibus decore vincimur.* We are excelled in comeliness by many living creatures: yea, of terrestrial creatures, that live with us. For, concerning those of the sea, omitting their figure, which no proportion can contain, so much doth it differ, both in colour, in neatness, in smoothness, and in disposition, we must give place unto them: which in all qualities we must likewise do to the airy ones. . . . Such as most resemble man are the vilest and filthiest of all the rout: As for outward appearance, it is the Monkey or Ape:

Simia quam similis, turpissima bestia, nobis!

as for inward and vital parts, it is the Hog. Truly, when I consider man all naked (yea, be it in that sex, which seemeth to have and challenge the greatest share of eye-pleasing beauty) and view his defects and manifold imperfections, I find we have had much more reason to hide and cover our nakedness than any creature else. We may be excused for borrowing those

which nature had there-in favoured more than us,
with their beauties to adorn us, and under their spoils
of wool, of hair, of feathers and of silk, to shroud us."

To shroud us . . . melancholy word. Remember,

> *Soon the grave must be your home,*
> *And your only suit, a shroud.*

Consider,

> *Green as the bay tree, ever green,*
>   *With its new foliage on,*
> *The gay, the thoughtless, have I seen,*
>   *I pass'd—and they were gone.*
>
> *Read, ye that run, the awful truth,*
>   *With which I charge my page;*
> *A worm is in the bud of youth,*
>   *And at the root of age.*

Having thus remembered and thus considered, I will
go out to my party in my new dress, gratulating myself that at least, if no handsomer than the ape, the
hog, and the hippopotamus, and rather less so than the
ant-eater, I have more wit than they, for I can, if
not make, anyhow cause to be made, and assume, a
flattering garment.

COWS

COWS

SEEN close, you would appear to have every fault but one. You are preposterously bovine, you are corniger-ous ruminants, you chew cud and let it dribble from your moving jaws, you stand in ruminating herds by stiles and gates, trampling the grass until it seems like the field of campaign at Passchendaal, fit for ducks, not men, to tread; you listlessly emit that pale, unencour-aging fluid which we offer to sick persons and young children and cats, and from which strong men and women turn in disgust; you pursue, with lowered horns, my dog. You are not beautiful; you are far from clean; and the melancholy cries with which you rend the evening skies are like steamers that take the ocean, or sirens in a fog.

What then is this strange pleasure that I take in your uncouth forms? What makes, as I approach you across the next field, my heart leap up as who beholds a rain-bow in the sky? Analysing it, I discern it to be a pleas-ure of sex. I have said that you have one virtue; my pleasure lies in perceiving it, in recognising that, what-ever you may have looked like from far, you are but cows after all.

But, alas, some of you are mothers: little ones run

at your sides; and it is of mothers alone among she-creatures that there is any truth in the otherwise preposterously mendacious statement that the female of the species is far deadlier than the male.

DEPARTURE OF VISITORS

DEPARTURE OF VISITORS

AN EXQUISITE peace obtains: a drowsy, golden peace, flowing honey-sweet over my dwelling, soaking it, dripping like music from the walls, strowing the floors like trodden herbs. A peace for gods; a divine emptiness.

> *Fair Quiet, have I found thee here,*
> *And Innocence, thy Sister dear!*
> *Mistaken long, I sought you then*
> *In busy Companies of Men. . . .*
> *Society is all but rude*
> *To this delicious Solitude.*

The easy chair spreads wide arms of welcome; the sofa stretches, guest-free; the books gleam, brown and golden, buff and blue and maroon, from their shelves; they may strew the floor, the chairs, the couch, once more, lying ready to the hand. "I am afraid the room is rather littered. . . ." The echo of the foolish words lingers on the air, is brushed away, dies forgotten, the air closes behind it. A heavy volume is heaved from its shelf on to the sofa. Silence drops like falling blossoms over the recovered kingdom from which pretenders have taken their leave.

What to do with all this luscious peace? It is a gift, a miracle, a golden jewel, a fragment of some gracious heavenly order, dropped to earth like some incredible strayed star. One's life to oneself again. Dear visitors, what largesse have you given, not only in departing, but in coming, that we might learn to prize your absence, wallow the more exquisitely in the leisure of your not-being.

To-night we shall sleep deep. We need no more hope that you "have everything you want"; we know that you have, for you are safely home, and can get it from your kitchen if you haven't. We send you blessing and God speed, and sink into our idle peace as into floods of down.

But you have unfortunately left behind you, besides peace, a fountain pen, a toothbrush, and a bottle of eye lotion with eye bath.

DISBELIEVING

DISBELIEVING

I BELIEVE very little: you will have to tell me something excessively credible before I believe it. Do not
come to me with your ghosts, crystals, palmistries,
cards, creeds, miracles, scandals, rumours, gossips, and
all the little news of the town; your new moons, black
cats, and piebald horses I cannot away with. Is there
an earthquake in the Barbadoes, an eruption in Sicily,
a war in Abyssinia, a revolution in Spain? It is possible:
but I do not see them, and have heard such tales
before.

I have a friend who cannot believe in atrocities. All
her life she has heard of atrocities, and earnestly sought
them when travelling abroad (for it is abroad that
atrocities occur), but she has been always disappointed,
for she has never found one. She was once told (says
she) of a Balkan atrocity exhibit, a woman of whom
it was reported that Bulgarian atrocities seen and suffered by her had made her mad, so that she was kept
in an asylum, a permanent exhibit. My friend, thinking, "Here is a veritable atrocity at last," made a pil-
grimage to the asylum and asked to see the woman,
but found her quite sane, only annoyed by her con-
finement. So now, when she hears of atrocities, she
always thinks of this woman whom atrocity had not

driven mad, and rejects them sadly. If you offer her past atrocities, such as those of Nero and Caligula, she rejects them too, feeling that Suetonius was unreliable. I do not go so far as this friend of mine; the atrociousness of human nature has not, I must conclude, been always without its vent. For my part, I decimate atrocities, which leaves me more than enough.

But, concerning most relations made to me, I consider, as Sir Thomas Browne held of the digesting of iron by the ostrich or sparrow-camel, that the negative seems most reasonably entertained. Or anyhow, whether reasonably or not, the most easily. Tell me what you will of earth or heaven; with Montaigne, I feel that we should say most times, there is no such matter.

It makes me feel agreeably aloof, not to be imposed on by all those strident, thundering events of which I hear, not to be taken in by rumour-mongers, magicians, gossips, quacks, moon's men, old wives' tales, "puerile hallucinations and anile delirations," and, in fact, the whole rumour of the humming world.

But sometimes a thought troubles me, and I ask myself, should I, many centuries back, have been numbered with those who denied the Antipodes, and the rotundity of earth? Of these Bishop Wilkins complained, mentioning among them Chrysostom, Austin, Lactantius, the Venerable Bede, Lucretius, Procopius, and the voluminous Abulensis, together with many Fathers, and with Herodotus, who wrote, "I cannot choose but laugh, to see so many men venture to describe the earth's compass, relating those things that are without all sense, as that the sea flows about the world, and that the Earth itself is round as an orb." While Lactantius exclaims, "What are they that think there are Antipodes, such as walk with their feet against ours? Is there anyone so foolish as to believe that there are men whose heels are higher than their heads, that the plants and trees grow downward? What shall we think, that men do cling like worms, or hang by their claws as cats?" with much other pleasantry such as the ignorant and unbelieving use.

I must beware, then, of too wide and too deep an incredulity, and remember that there are many things yet hid from us, and that really everything is extremely peculiar.

DOVES IN THE CHIMNEY

DOVES IN THE CHIMNEY

THE voice of the turtle is heard in my chimney. It is the prettiest soft low crooning in the world, like the soughing of wind in a pine wood, or the low moan of seas imprisoned between rocks. When first it stole into my room, as I sat reading there, I thought I had been Steele's pastoral lady friend, Mrs. Cornelia Lizard, "whose Head was so far turned . . . that she kept a Pair of Turtles cooing in her Chamber, and had a tame Lamb running after her up and down the House. I used all gentle Methods to bring her to her self. . . ."

But no: I am more fortunate that Mrs. Cornelia, not only in that I am lambless, but in that my pair of turtles, (if pair they are, and not a mourning widow turtling it after her mate) have not taken up their abode in my chamber, but have, it seems, made them a nest in my chimney. Yes, my chimney is a pigeon-cote, a culver-house, and in it the kind turtles sit and coo, and answer to each other's moan. I like to think that there are two turtles, that my turtle is not bereaved. And yet, to have so chaste, so musically mourning a widow at hand, would also be charming. "As a turtle-dove did I chatter, and as a dove did I mourn"; melancholy ordinance of nature, that this otherwise oblivious bird, so unlike the elephant that she forgets practically everything immediately, including her young the moment they have been taken from the nest, and the peckings and unkindnesses of her husband, and all wrongs done her, should remember and mourn her mate until death. Even the widowed cock mourns, winging him to some withered bough, or to some friendly chimney. But who shall say why he mourns? Basil wrote that the eating of vipers, a favourite food of theirs, gives turtles a pain, until they can find some marjoram to heal it. They will find no marjoram in my chimney, and so they mourn there still.

But no; I believe that turtles have been misjudged, and that the gentle crooning which has been taken to indicate grief actually, even in the solitary bird, expresses a tranquil pleasure in existence. I like to think this, for I have (who can other?) a great esteem for this amiable bird, so kind, so passing chaste, a messenger of peace, an ensample of simpleness, clean, plenteous in children, follower of meekness, friend of company, forgetter of wrongs, nicely curious, carrier of letters, emblem of the Holy Ghost. I will not suppose that my chimney-cole culver is a sad widow; she is the most constant pretty cooing turtle, and doubtless a happy, if forgetful, mother, sitting upon an ill-made nest up there and crooning to her unborn turtlets. Her voice is so sweet, so comforting, so heavenly, it would convert the sceptical *jeune homme de Dijon* himself, did he hear it as I hear it now, rising, murmuring, falling, dying, melting away to start again—croo, croo, croo.

My chimney is a hospitable lodging for turtles. But what is their fate when they make their home in chimneys which are funnels for fire and smoke? Do they flit away, forgetting their turtlets, at the first alarm, to build in the next chimney? Or do they remain, faithful birds, amid the choking fumes, until, like the Phœnix and the Turtle, they enclosed in cinders lie?

DRIVING A CAR

DRIVING A CAR

To PROPEL a car through space, to devour the flying miles, to triumph over roads, flinging them behind us like discarded snakes, to rush, like Mulciber, from morn to noon, from noon to dewy eve, a summer's day, up hill and down, by singing fir woods and blue heath, annihilating counties and minifying kingdoms—here is a joy that Phaethon, that bad driver, never knew. Phaethon, like us, was inebriated with rushing (as he fondly thought) through the air, intoxicated with pride in the great and hazardous car he drove, deeming himself a speed king. He believed himself to be doing his circuit of 583 million miles in twenty-four hours, or about 25,000,000 m.p.h. That is to say, had the sun really been rushing daily round the earth, that is about what it would have had to do, though it is possible that neither Helios nor Phaethon actually knew the mileage. Anyhow, as we now know, Phaethon was not really moving at all; it was the earth that was moving, and Phaethon crashed simply from nerves.

The same might be said of all the charioteers before the present age; they thought they were speeding, but were really scarcely moving at all. Nero fancied himself as a driver: but what was Nero doing? At the most, about fifteen. Bishop Wilkins much praised for their swiftness certain chariots with wheels and sails that were, said he, driven over land by the wind at a rate far exceeding the swiftness of ships on the sea. Such chariots sailed, he said, over the great smooth plains of China; and there was one at Sceveling in Holland, which that eminent inquisitive man Peireskius travelled to see, and would ever after talk of it, saying that its passengers did not feel the motion of the wind that drove them, since they travelled with equal speed themselves; men running before it seemed to go backwards, and things which seemed at a great distance were presently overtaken and left behind. Grotius was very copious and elegant in the celebration of this invention, and Bishop Wilkins inquires, what could be more delightful than to make use of the wind, which costs nothing and eats nothing, instead of horses. In two hours' space, says he, the Sceveling chariot would travel two and forty miles. So, after all this fuss and travelling to see it and excitement on the part of English bishops and the eminent inquisitive Peireskius and the copious elegant Grotius, the thing could only do twenty-one.

The fact that our grandchildren, nay, our children, will soon be talking with similar contempt of us, rather adds to than detracts from our pleasure. The cars that we send hurtling over the earth by the touch of a foot on a knob are but at the beginning of their race with time and space; we drive slow and clumsy embryos. But they are swift enough to delight us, as with open throttle and hands lightly on the wheel we scud the roads, watching the needle mount, slipping past those other cars which unfortunately also scud the roads and impede our view.

All is bliss; we hum songs of triumph, as all charioteers have, even when they have been ignobly dragged by the brute creation, instead of by a drop of volatile spirit and a rotating engine, which is so obviously far better. Our song is chorused by the little chirping squeak of the door handles, the faint rattling of the windows, the less faint humming of the engine, the running of the wind. The scenery is doubled in charm by being seen at this rate; it flashes by with the vividness of a string of jewels, glimpsed, admired, and gone. How tired we should get of it were we afoot, trudging along with pack on back! One should not give scenery the chance to fatigue one. Seen thus, it will glow in the memory like a fairy land scarce trodden, awaiting one's return.

The serpent in this Eden, the canker in this lovely bloom of speed, is (need one say it?) the other vehicles in our road. And particularly in the middle of our road, which is where cars, horse-carts, and cyclists love to travel. But, did all travellers keep, as they should, to their near side, driving would be too like heaven for sinful man below. As it is, when our time comes to go, when we fall in turn to the juggernaut, we may hope to be translated to some paradise traversed by great fair roads, to each soul a road to herself, along which her car shall dash at some supramundane speed, hugging (for souls shall be made perfect) the near border of thymey Elysian grass.

EASTER IN THE WOODS

EASTER IN THE WOODS

A DELICATE shimmer of greenery flickers, a light veil, over purple and brown, and starry blackthorn and wild cherry-blossom riot, in flights gay and white like angels, over wood and hill. How the copses, all enverdured with larch and birch and thorn and springing beech, climb the steep brown hillsides, running down to cowslipped dells and banks, while at their feet the marshy bottoms, gold-starred with kingcups, lie! Standing here, my feet deep in brown beech leaves, on Wheatham Hill's steep shoulder, I can see the high hangers, copses, valleys, commons and farms, for miles around. There is the long, circling hanger called, in its different curves, Oakshott, Juniper, and Happersnapper, lying coiled, like a great snake of beech and oak, holly and birch, and alder, on the heights above Higher, Middle, and Lower Oakshott Farms; there are Moore's Copse, Cheesecombe, Cherrycombe, lying about Oakshott Stream to the north; in the nearer distance burgeon those three petty copses, Roundabout, Hazel Holt, and Naps. While to the south writhes the wild steep Shoulder-of-Mutton hill, all embeeched, and edged along the ridge, where the wood breaks into bare grass gnarled with wind-bent thorn-trees, by the little deep-set path of Cockshut

Lane. Eastward, in the near distance between the meadowy valley below these woods where I stand, and the running line of high moor and forest beyond, Wheatham Farm lies on its hill; its hens have laid Easter eggs, and their cries of content float to me through the soft still air, striking their own exotic galline note in the merry Easter concert that pours from the greenwood. What plumy people sing in every grove! What whistling, what warbling, what chiff-chaffing, what lyric sopranos and coloraturas, what shrill sweet zest! Could humanity but sing like this. . . .

But I am waiting and listening for a voice overdue, a voice as yet unheard by me this year. Will it come to-day? The stage is all adorned and set for the entry of this monotonous but enchanting performer; here is blossom and greenwood, soft sunshine and blue shadow, light breezes and sweet air. But he tarries still. The stone-chat ejaculates, sharp and bright, from the furzy common; the wheat-ear nods and flirts and says "Chak chak"; the ring ouzel sings, wild and gay, doing, no doubt, his marriage dance in the patch of moory grass above the wood; the blackbird, already settled, a householder, mellowly and with prosperous dignity whistles a tune; the nightingale jugs, the robin warbles, the wren twees, the goldcrest (or is it a long-tailed tit?) zee-zee-zees, the Dartford Warbler pittews, the hedge-sparrow chirrups, the linnet trills. At least, this is what I believe that I am hearing; the sum of it, anyhow, is the finest merry melodious canticling you can hear in a Hampshire Easter week.

And then, from the brown heart of Roundabout Copse, breaks the cry, high, far and clear, of the roving bully who is just arrived for his season of pleasure and increase in these islands after his African tour, and carelessly brags the freedom of himself and spouse from household cares, from the tedium of domesticity, from the trouble of parenthood, from the monotony of monogamy. The cuckoo is a witty bird; hearing his gay, cool, exultant cry, one hails once more the eternal pleasurist. They know how to live, these cuckoos; they rove, they love (briefly, but effectively), they breed, they procreate, they lay their cheerful Easter eggs singly in homes of eggs like-hued, relying, with a confidence justified by the inherited experience of ages, on the frail intellects and kind hearts of non-cuculan birds; and so away to the greenwood they hie, having thus made ample and painless provision for a progeny they have no notion of ever seeing again. Family business thus brilliantly disposed of, all spring and summer stretches before them for song, riot and debauchery; and why in the world their name has been taken by humanity as a synonym for stupidity, passes conjecture. Wise birds; intelligent, unscrupulous, cynical, sensible birds, wearing their freedom like a panache, crying it like a witty brag. They seem to me to have a Renaissance touch, to be like Medici princes and popes, luxurious, clever, conscienceless, getting the better of simpler, better men and women, looting the world of its pleasures and giving in return only their own insolent enjoyment. Life is no trouble to cuckoos;

solvitur cantando. Their gay boast rings over the April woods like bells, ringing in the merry summer. First far, then drifting nearer, from Roundabout to Hazel Holt, from Hazel Holt to Naps Copse, and so across the dell to Wheatham Hanger, and then all over and about the wood, *cuckoo, cuckoo, cuckoo,* so negligently, boldly gay, as if they mocked, as well as they may, the chorus of little warblers, the future foster-parents of their, as yet, unlaid young. *Cuckoo, cuckoo, cuckoo!* the cry drifts westward, away and away towards Juniper Hanger. Follow it through the greening woods, up sweet dim twisting paths, among the alders and the great bare budding beeches and the young slim beeches springing green, rustling through the deep brown pile of the beech carpet (laid last autumn, and overlaid with the green running pattern of agrimony), by ancient chalk pits and blown bare ridges hawthorn-grown, across the deep grass track of Old Litten Lane, and so to the wild sweep of Juniper Hanger, where it climbs above the Oakshotts against a shifting, sea-hued sky. The cuckoo is away now, following his private ploys somewhere in Happersnapper woods, but he has left the spring behind him, its gay bravery and the eternal dip-and-come-up of the dauntless, resurrecting Easter world, with its cowslips, its singing, and its dancing sun.

But now the blue distances deepen to violet; rain sweeps across the Oakshotts from Selborne way, and patters light drops on the beeches. Decoyed from wood to wood by the teasing gay bird, as if by the tee-heeing pixies, I am left now deserted by it as by these, with the Easter rain pattering on holt and hanger, and the chorus of good little birds warbling and weeting on every bough.

EATING AND DRINKING

EATING AND DRINKING

HERE is a wonderful and delightful thing, that we should have furnished ourselves with orifices, with traps that open and shut, through which to push and pour alien objects that give us such pleasurable, such delicious sensations, and at the same time sustain us. A simple pleasure; a pleasure accessible, in normal circumstances and in varying degrees, to all, and that several times each day. An expensive pleasure, if calculated in the long run and over a lifetime; but count the cost of each mouthful as it comes, and it is (naturally) cheaper. You can, for instance, get a delicious plate of spaghetti and cheese, or fried mushrooms and onions, for very little; or practically anything else, except caviare, smoked salmon, the eggs of plovers, ostriches and humming-birds, and fauna and flora completely out of their appropriate seasons, which you will, of course, desire, but to indulge such desires is Gluttony, or Gule, against which the human race has always been warned. It was, of course, through Gule that our first parents fell. As the confessor of Gower's Amans told him, this vice of gluttony was in Paradise, most deplorably mistimed.

We shall never know what that fruit was, which so solicited the longing Eve, which smelt so savoury, which tasted so delightful as greedily she ingorged it without restraint. The only fruit that has ever seemed to me to be worthy of the magnificently inebriating effects wrought by its consumption on both our parents is the mango. When I have eaten mangoes, I have felt like Eve.

> *Satiate at length,*
> *And hightn'd as with Wine, jocond and boon,*
> *Thus to her self she pleasingly began.*
> *O sovran, vertuous, precious of all trees*
> *In Paradise, of operation blest. . . .*

And like both of them together:

As with new Wine intoxicated both
They swim in mirth, and fansie that they feel
Divinitie within them breeding wings
Wherewith to scorn the Earth: but that false Fruit
Farr other operation first displaid. . . .

And so on. But, waking up the morning after mangoes, one does not feel such ill effects as was produced by that fallacious fruit when its exhilarating vapour bland had worn off. One feels, unless one has very grossly exceeded, satiate, happy and benign, turning sweet memories over on one's palate, desiring, for the present, no more of anything. The part of the soul (see Timæus) which desires meats and drinks lies torpid and replete by its manger, somewhere between midriff and navel, for there the gods housed these desires, that wild animal chained up with man, which must be nourished if man is to exist, but must not be allowed to disturb the council chamber, the seat of reason. For the authors of our race, said Timæus, were aware that we should be intemperate in eating and drinking, and take a good deal more than was necessary or proper, by reason of gluttony. Prescient and kindly authors of our race! What a happy companion they allotted to mankind in this wild animal, whom I should rather call a domestic and pampered pet. How sweet it is to please it, to indulge it with delicious nourishment, with superfluous tit-bits and pretty little tiny kick-shaws, with jellies, salads, dainty fowls and fishes, fruits and wines and pasties, fattened and entruffled livers of geese, sturgeon's eggs from Russia, salmon from the burn, omelettes and soufflés from the kitchen. I have always thought the Glutton in Piers Plowman a coarse and unresourceful fellow, who, on his way to church and shrift, was beguiled merely by a brewer-ess's offer of ale. (How ungenteel Mr. H. W. Fowler must have thought her, and all of her century and many later centuries, for using this word, which he so condemns, for beer!) The Glutton asked, had she also any hot spices? and she assured him that she had pep-per, paeony seeds, garlic, and fennel. And with this simple and unpleasing fare, Glutton was content, and made merry globbing it until night. Glutton was no gourmet, no Lucullus. Nothing recked he of rare and dainty dishes; nothing out of the ordinary entered his imagination. Not for him the spitted lark, the artful sauce, the delicate salad of chopped herbs and frogs.

There are some sad facts concerning eating and drinking. One is that the best foods are unwholesome: an arrangement doubtless made by the authors of our being in order to circumvent gluttony. It is a melancholy discovery made early by infants, and repeatedly by adults. We all have to make it in turn, only excepting the ostrich. No doubt the Lady in Comus made it later, after she had more fully grown up, though as an adolescent we find her remarking, sententiously and erroneously, to the enticing sorcerer,

> *And that which is not good is not delicious*
> *To a well-govern'd and wise appetite.*

Even the untutored savage knows better than this. They of Dominica, said Antonio de Herrera, that elegant Castilian chronicler of Spanish travels in the West Indies, they of Dominica did eat, one day, a Friar, but he proved unwholesome, and all who partook were ill, and some died, and therefore they of Dominica have left eating human flesh. This was a triumph for Friars, which must be envied by many of the animal world.

Another sad comestive truth is that the best foods are the products of infinite and wearying trouble. The trouble need not be taken by the consumer, but someone, ever since the Fall, has had to take it. Even raw fruit was, to the exiles from Eden, hard to come by.

Their meanest simple cheer (says Sylvester)
Our wretched parents bought full hard and deer.
To get a Plum, sometimes poor Adam rushes
With thousand wounds among a thousand bushes.
If they desire a Medler for their food,
They must go seek it through a fearfull wood;
Or a brown Mulbery, then the ragged Bramble
With thousand scratches doth their skin bescramble.

And, did they desire anything better, they could not have it at all. Slowly they learned, we suppose, about planting seeds and reaping ears and grinding flour and welding it into that heavy substance we call bread. Rather more quickly, perhaps, about the merits of dead animals as food, but how long it took them to appreciate the niceties of cooking these, we know not. That is to say, no doubt the students of the history of man know, but I do not.

Once learnt, this business of cooking was to prove an ever growing burden. It scarcely bears thinking about, the time and labour that man and womankind has devoted to the preparation of dishes that are to melt and vanish in a moment like smoke or a dream, like a shadow, and as a post that hastes by, and the air closes behind them, and afterwards no sign where they went is to be found.

Still, one must keep one's head, and remember that some people voluntarily undertake these immense and ephemeral labours, for pay or for a noble love of art even at its most perishable, or from not being able to think of a way of avoiding it. All honour to these slaves of baked-meats: let them by all means apply themselves to their labours; so long as those who do not desire to prepare food are not compelled to do so. If you are of these, and can get no one to cook for you in your home, you should eat mainly such objects as are sold in a form ready for the mouth, such as cheese, bread, butter, fruit, sweets, dough-nuts, macaroons, meringues, and everything that comes (if you have a tin-opener) out of tins. If you can endure to apply a very little and rudimentary trouble to the matter yourself, eggs are soon made ready, even by the foolish; bacon also. I would not advise you to attempt real meat; this should only be cooked by others; so should potatoes.

But, whatever has been prepared for you, and who-ever has had the ill chance to prepare it, there comes the exquisite moment when you push or pour it into the mouth. What bliss, to feel it rotating about the palate, being chewed (if this is required) by the teeth, slipping, in chewed state, down the throat, down the gullet, down the body to the manger, there to find its temporary home. Or, if it is liquid, to feel it gurgling and gushing, like the flood of life, quite down the throat with silver sound, running sweet ichor through the veins. Red wine, golden wine, pink wine, ginger beer (with gin or without), the juice of grape-fruit or orange, tea, coffee, chocolate, iced soda from the fountain, even egg nogg—how merrily and like to brooks they run!

My subject runs away with me: I could, had I but

time and space, discourse on it for ever. I could mention the great, the magnificent gourmets of history; I could dwell on the pleasures experienced by Lucullus, Heliogobalus, those Roman Emperors, those English monarchs, those Aldermen, who, having dined brilliantly and come to sad satiety, had their slaves tickle them with feathers behind the ears until this caused them to retire in haste from the table, to which they presently returned emptied and ready to work through the menu again. These are the world's great gluttons; to them eating and drinking was a high art.

But they are beaten by one Nicholas Wood, a yeoman of Kent, who, in the reign of James I, "did eat with ease a whole sheep of 16 shillings price, and that raw, at one meal; another time he eat 13 dozen of pigeons. At Sir William Sedley's he eat as much as would have sufficed 30 men; at the Lord Wotton's in Kent, he eat at one meal 84 rabbits, which number would have sufficed 168 men, allowing to each half a rabbit. He suddenly devoured 18 yards of black pudding, London measure, and having once eat 60 lbs. weight of cherries, he said, they were but wastemeat. He made an end of a whole hog at once, and after it swallowed three pecks of damsons; this was after breakfast, for he said he had eat one pottle of milk, one pottle of pottage, with bread, butter, and cheese, before. He eat in my presence, saith Taylor, the water poet, six penny wheaten loaves, three sixpenny veal pies, one pound of sweet butter, one good dish of thornback, and a sliver of a peck household loaf, an inch thick, and all this within the space of an hour: the house yielded no more, so he went away unsatisfied. . . . He spent all his estate to provide for his belly; and though a landed man, and a true labourer, he died very poor in 1630."

And this is the third snag about good eating and drinking.

Nevertheless, expensive, troublesome, and unwholesome though it be, it is a pleasure by no means to be forgone.

ELEPHANTS IN BLOOMSBURY

ELEPHANTS IN BLOOMSBURY

CAN it be true, or do I dream? Driving at dead of the night (if the night is ever dead) through Tavistock Square, can it be that I discern in the street before me a herd of elephants? Large, grey, tranquil, accompanied by a man with a little stick, I think that I see them pad along the Bloomsbury streets, swinging their heads, their trunks, this way and that, enjoying the air of the cool summer night. Slowly I drive past them; they do not seem concerned. I leave them behind; I see them mirrored in my glass, padding, wagging, pompous, serene, wreathing their lithe proboscis to make me mirth, as if they trod their native jungle tracks.

Native? Were elephants, after all, not native to these islands once? Did they not roam our tangled weald and jungled swamps, trumpeting blithely one to another as cows in pastures trumpet now? Have they, perhaps, never quite vanished, and do they still pad out on a summer night to take the air, tramping round our pleasant squares, breaking off boughs from the trees in the gardens and munching them, one little eye ever open for their bitter foe the dragon? Does the she-elephant go seeking in vain for the mandragora tree, that her husband may eat thereof and turn to her and give her the little elephants which she, never (it is said) he, intermittently craves? And when these little creatures are due, does she pad Thamesward, along the Embankment, seeking steps down into the river, that she may bear them in water, safely out of reach of the dragon? And do the herd go thither always to drink? for they drink not wine, we are told, except in wartime, when they like to get drunk, but will suck up whole rivers of water, and it must be muddy, for they will not drink if they see their own shadow therein.

I recall other things I have heard about elephants: how they hate mice, love sweet flowers, which they will go gathering in baskets, and will not eat the food in their stables until they have decked the mangers with these fragrant nosegays and herbs. I recall how chaste they are, how never there is adultery among them; how they love and defend their young; how, though like to living mountains in quantity, no little dog becomes more serviceable and tractable; how the African elephant has such an inferiority complex that if he do but see an Indian one he trembles and hurries past, by all means to get out of his sight.

I think of their patriotism, how they love their own countries so well that they will not go abroad unless their rulers swear a solemn oath that they shall return; and, even after this, and however well entertained they be with meats and pleasures abroad, they will always weep. The elephants I have just passed were not, I think, weeping; they must, therefore, be native to this land.

I remember how, when they have eaten a chameleon by mistake with their leaves, they will die unless immediately they take a wild olive; how they are so loving to their fellows that they will not eat alone, but invite each other to their feasts, like reasonable civil men; how the troglodytes take them by leaping on to their backs from trees and shooting them with arrows dipped in serpent's gall; how at the new moon they come together in great companies and bathe in rivers and lout one to another, and teach their children to do likewise; how if they meet a man lost in the wilderness, they will draw themselves out of the way, not to affright him, and then will pass before him and show him his road; how they will face and overthrow troops in battle, but will flee from the least sound of a swine; how, like the unicorn, they love young maidens, and when these sing will come and listen until they fall asleep.

Other of their amiable habits come to my mind: how they are excellent linguists, and understand human tongues; how they remember their duties, delight in love, glory, goodness, honesty, prudence, and equity; how religiously they reverence the sun, moon, planets and stars; how they can learn the most ingenious tricks, such as climbing up ropes and sliding down head first, and flinging darts into the air.

Yea (if the Grecians do not mis-recite)
With's crooked trumpet he doth sometimes write.

Great dancers they are too, though sometimes in a somewhat rude and disorderly manner; and marvellous bashful, and die easily of shame; it does not do to make game of elephants; they never, as is well known, forget. I recall also how great conquerors have always used them—Hannibal in the Alps; Alexander; Bacchus, who charioted over India behind a pair of them; Pompey, who returned, similarly encharioted, to Rome after the conquest of Africa, but his elephants failed to pass two abreast through the gates.

All these feats and characters of elephants I recall, and more beside, as I drive home through the bland, lit streets of London. Elephants become, as I brood on them, so wonderful, so all that I admire, looming heaven-high, far more than brute and little less than god, that by the time I reach the British Museum I am sure that I never saw elephants straying free in Tavistock Square. They were ghosts, dreams, no more flesh and blood than the two lions who guard the Museum's back door. I think of them as the historian of Ophirian travels thought of elephants in Peru. No Elephant said he, could come into Peru but by miracle, the cold and high hills every way encompassing being impassable to that creature. Yea, said he, I aver further that an Elephant could not live in Peru, but by miracle. For the hills are cold in extremity and the valleys without water, whereas the Elephant delights in places very hot and very moist. But I deserve blame, he concludes, to fight with Elephants in America, which is less than a shadow, and to lay siege to Castles in the Air.

Less than a shadow. Perhaps my nocturnal elephants in Bloomsbury were, after all, no more than that. Nevertheless, I swear they moved, mighty and gentle and elephant-grey, swinging heavy heads and wreathing lithe trunks, across Tavistock Square an hour before the midsummer dawn.

And really, if the London traffic problem is going now to be complicated by elephants, heaven alone knows where it will all end. We shall be having dinosaurs next.

FASTEST ON EARTH

FASTEST ON EARTH

When I return to my parked car, I often find on it, attached to the wind-screen or window or lying on the seat, a square of paper bearing the printed boast, "Fastest on Earth." I should like to keep it there, a visible testimony to my car's prowess, as I roll through the streets, that other cars, yes, and even omnibuses, may yield to me and my Morris pride of place in the Hyde Park Corner scuffle, at the Marble Arch round-about, and dashing up Baker Street. "There goes," they would say, "the Atalanta among cars; see how it swifts along, passing all others; it travels post, it shoots through space like a star, or would, were it not held up by other traffic and by policemen; it is the car of Mercury himself, make way, make way!" The dogs would bark, the children scream, up fly the windows all, and every soul cry out, "Well done!" as loud as he could bawl. "She carries weight, she rides a race! 'Tis for a thousand pound!" And still, as fast as I drew near, 'twas wonderful to view how in a trice the turnpike-men their gates wide open threw. Gongs would sound, police shout, all would be uproar and pursuit.

The very thought of going thus tagged and bragged, intoxicates, weights my foot on the accelerator, speeds my swift course around St. James's Square.

But see, he who tagged me hastens up; he appears to desire remuneration. He is also informing me that I have left my car in his park for over two hours. "Fastest on Earth" indeed, when I cannot even hurry out of the square quickly enough not to be overtaken by one of its covetous and curmudgeonly guardians. So much for his label; I scatter it to the winds.

FINISHING A BOOK

FINISHING A BOOK

IT IS done, it is over. This litter of papers that has got in my way, taking my time and my space and my energy, intruding on my leisure, for so many months, this horrid mess of nonsense which I call a book—do it up in brown paper, send it away to its publisher, let me see it no more. Let me not look ahead. For the moment, I have rid me of its foolish presence, and that is enough.

Leisure spreads before my dazzled eyes, a halcyon sea, too soon to be cumbered with the flotsam and jetsam of purposes long neglected, which will, I know it, drift quickly into view again once I am embarked upon that treacherous, enticing ocean. Leisure now is but a brief business, and past return are the days when it seemed to stretch, blue and unencumbered, between one occupation and the next. There are always arrears, always things undone, doubtless never to be done, putting up teasing, reproachful heads, so that, although I slug, I slug among the wretched souls whom care doth seek to kill. But now, just emerged as I am from the tangled and laborious thicket which has so long embosked me, I will contemplate a sweet and unencumbered slugging, a leisure and a liberty as of lotus eaters or gods. As for books, never more will I write one;

nay, I have done, you get no more of me. Is there none other way by which I may sustain a life, own a roof-tree, a bed, a board, a car, a few clothes? Must I depend on these accursed labours, these toils that never cease?

Forget them. This last bundle of them has taken to itself wings like a dove; it will flee away and leave me at rest.

But, alas, it is a homing pigeon; it will return to me, typed words turned into print, bristling with even more errors, even more solecisms and follies, than when it left my hands. I shall struggle laboriously to amend it, send it away once more, and it will again return to make a fool of me in the end.

FIRE ENGINES

FIRE ENGINES

How they dash by, car after car, brave in scarlet,
imperious with clanging bells, fraught with an army
of courageous brass-helmed men! What calm and
placid-seeming beings! And yet they must be seeth-
ing, beneath that tranquil exterior, beneath those
bright helmets, with more than all the excitement of
those who go to look at fires, for they are pyromachs,
they will wage a fearful war with ravening flames,
they will run up ladders and rescue human beings,
furniture, and cats from incineration, they will turn
on a hose and deluge rooms and buildings with cooling,
quenching streams, watched from all sides by a gratified populace and a busily recording Press.

All this, at least, is what I suppose that they mean
to do when they arrive at the destination towards
which they are so rapidly and impetuously proceed-
ing, admitting no obstacle, ignoring traffic signals,
ringing an imperious peal which sends cars, omnibuses,
pedestrians, cyclists, yes, even horse-vans, those stately,
marching monarchs of the street, scuttling out of their
way.

So, one imagines, did the chariots of Roman Con-
suls dash imperiously, clatteringly, through Roman
streets, scattering Roman citizens as the white herds

on the mountains and in the chestnut-shadowed gorges scatter before wolves. Did the Roman citizens, thus scattered, gaze on the speeding chariots with applause and exultation in their hearts, with that joyful yet lachrymose emotion which is caused by the sight of rapidly speeding brass-helmed men with coiled lengths of hose, jangling bells as they hurry flame-ward in flame-hued cars? No; our emotion must be more pleasurable, for it is fiery in origin; paradoxically, it is pyrolatry which causes us to delight in these pyroletrous engines and men.

Not only pyroletrous but panolethrous, for their scarlet cars of Juggernaut mow down all that cannot expeditiously enough fly from their path, and one of them has grazed my car's newly painted wing. I make no protest; they would not heed me were I to do so. They are out on a practice run and no casualties shall give them pause.

FLATTERY

FLATTERY

How rare, how sweet they fall, these honeyed words, these golden bells that stroke the listening air! O Flattery, thou coaxing, heav'nly maid, thou com'st too seldom to seduce and soothe. How amiable are thy feet as thou drawest nigh, how bright and insincere thy smile!

Sometimes the post brings thee. Perhaps an American professor has written me a kind word; he is learned as well as good-natured; he seems to know what is good in literature. Perhaps it is, instead, a kindly unknown, living in the English provinces. What a clever, well-educated man! What a sympathetic, intelligent woman! How different from some others! Here is someone who admires my poetry; another who thinks my essays well expressed; even my novels well conceived, with passable plots. Their words are sweet as honey in the mouth. An author there are few to praise should save and keep these copious and elegant celebrations of her merit: keep them, and show them one day to those contemners, those heapers of gratuitous obloquy, who write tasteless and tactless books pointing out how deficient in literary merit and personal worth practically all authors are. Here, Mr. Blank (I shall say), is the real truth about me, which you, who have apparently omitted to read the majority of my works before pronouncing on them and on me, have so blindly overlooked. What about this, pray, I shall boast to the reviewers of my next book, when they find it insubstantial and facetious, or pedantic and dull, or sadly trivial and unconvincing. I would like you to know (I shall say) what this learned professor thinks of me, and this excellent gentleman from (or perhaps still in) Yorkshire, and all these ardent young students who desire to write a thesis on me in German, Italian, French and Scandinavian universities. (This is not a form of flattery that pleases me, as these young innocents all request lengthy and informing answers, and, though from me they receive no answer, they remain, on account of their projected theses and their tender years, a little on my conscience. It is obvious that they write to all authors. Has any so far answered them, poor nit-wits?)

Flattery. That great call, to which every sentient being down the ages has responded. Gods, men, women, children, beasts and birds; how readily these have fallen into the snares spread for their feet, the while they spruce themselves and smirk and smug, tripping it along life's highway, toes barely touching the earth, as if they were indeed puffed up with these agreeable gases until they have acquired the levity of balloons. For a very little, they would leave the earth, and soar away into the skyey sphere, still smiling and smirking like cherubs among the buxom clouds. "Vix humum tetigit pede," wrote Milton of his proud and dreaming youth; scarcely did he touch the earth with his feet; and so these happy ones who live with flattery. The sweet inebriant only comes my way on occasion, and stays not long enough to obliviate that negligence which is man's normal earthly portion. I would that it were otherwise. I would wish to go companioned and beleaguered by flatterers telling their sugared lies, like those Italian gentlemen whom one meets in trains. "Come è bellina, simpatica, graziosa!" Charming voices murmur in one's memory, like honeybees among clover. How comely and how elegant you appear, how fitly garbed, how altogether worthy of esteem. Nor man nor woman did I ever see, at all parts equal to the parts in thee. . . .

"Think'st thou," asked Silvia disagreeably of Protheus trying to please her, "think'st thou I am so shallow, so conceitless, to be seduced by thy flattery?" "Nay, Sir," says Dr. Johnson, "flattery pleases very generally. In the first place, the flatterer may think what he says to be true: but in the second place, whether he thinks so or not, he certainly thinks those whom he flatters of consequence enough to be flattered." In the third place, he has a kindly desire to please them, and they are churlish indeed if they be not pleased by his amiable intentions, his delightful cozenage. Look on the pleasant fellow's picture, sketched three centuries since by the observant but hard-to-please Dr. John Earle.

"He will commend to you first what he knows you like, and has always some absurd story or other of your enemy. . . . He will ask your counsel some-times as a man of deep judgment . . . and whatso-ever you say, is persuaded. . . . A piece of wit bursts him with an overflowing laughter, and he remem-bers it for you to all companies, and laughs again in the telling. He is one never chides you but for your virtues, as, *you are too good, too honest, too religious*. . . . It is a happiness not to discover him, for as long as you are happy, you shall not."

Certainly I shall not. By all means flatter me; be kind and courteous; hop in my walks and gambol in my eyes; feed me with apricocks and dewberries; nod to me and do me courtesies, fool me to the top of my bent, for I enjoy it.

Though, alas, it makes the unflattering world at large seem more hard, chilly and malicious than ever.

FLOWER SHOP IN THE NIGHT

FLOWER SHOP IN THE NIGHT

How it glows, golden lit, empty of people, mysterious and dumb, behind curved glass that is as space bending unseen, that melts into the still, thin air, guarding what seems to the deceived eye unguarded and free to the touch. Still and bright and strange, like a deserted fairyland, like Eden after its erred denizens had been outed, like a palace garden whence queens have fled, gleams that ordered and enchanted space, blossoming like a greenhouse in the dead of the night. Golden baskets are piled high with pink roses; crimson roses riot in curious jars; hydrangeas make massed rainbows beneath many-coloured lights; tall lilies form a frieze behind, like liveried, guarding angels. Among the flowers are piled exotic fruits, pears and pines and medlars, little round fruitlets from China; clusters of purple grapes, asparagus in close formation, pressed together like sardines reared on end.

It is all very lovely, this gleaming vision of the night, so still, remote and bright, entranced behind its unseen glass, as it were a water garden deep planted in green seas, lit by the phosphorent illumination of a thousand fish. And look, it has glass tanks of fish, coral, and sea horses, softly shining in each corner, sending faint light over the flower garden from below, while brighter lights illustrate it from the high walls.

It is a scene so exquisite and so strange that it might be a mirage, to melt away before the wondering gaze. We will leave it, while it is still clear and brilliant; turn away and walk down the cold, empty and echoing street, looking not back lest that bright garden be darkened and fled like a dream before dawn.

FLYING

FLYING

I AM in the cockpit of the Klemm two-seater of my friend. I am helmeted, goggled, strapped in. There was recently a man not strapped in, says my cheerful friend, as he takes his place behind me, who got left in the air two thousand feet up when the plane dropped in a pocket. The man followed, quickly but inaccurately; he reached the earth first. So it is better to be strapped in.

We taxy (odd word for it) over green pastures and turn into the wind. The starting light shines in the tower, the throttle is opened full, the engine roars. Faster and faster we go, bounce once or twice, and suddenly are off the meadow, in the air, rising up, climbing th'aerial height with eager haste, winging it like the mounting lark, scaling the steep ascent of heaven like the saints, eager to be above the clouds. What height now, I shout through my telephone to the pilot behind. About a thousand, he calls back. To be above the clouds we must climb two thousand more.

Still we fly sunward, like Icarus the rash. We are in the clouds now, pushing through them, flying blind. I, in my intrepidity, am unmoved by this; the pilot does not share my nonchalance, as he believes

223

the heavens to be cluttered with hidden aeroplanes practising from the school. The clouds are cool and wet; when we emerge from them the wind-screens are seen to be soaked and dripping, as if we had been in a storm of rain.

We are above them now, winging through a heaven of sunshine, with cushiony billows floating below, a feather bed for the gods, a range of snowy mountains, a forest of giant white trees, a pride of fairy castles, a gibbering of gliding, shrouding ghosts, a field of ice. Through rifts and chasms we catch glimpses of a distant earth, laid out green and hedged, like a chequerboard.

How high now?

About four thousand.

We speed along through radiant space. Enormous bliss, as Milton would say.

How fast? I call.

About a hundred miles.

It does not feel that, with only thin air for resistance. A car travelling at forty seems faster. Until you put a hand outside the wind-screen; then the whole weight and force of the heavens rushes storming against you.

We are nosing downward now; we shall soon be below the clouds again; we fly earthward, as the Archangel Raphael flew from heaven.

Down thither prone in flight
He speeds, and through the vast ethereal sky

Sails between worlds and worlds, with steady wing
Now on the polar winds, then with quick fan
Winnows the buxom air; till, within soar
Of towering eagles, to all the fowls he seems
A Phœnix, gazed by all as that sole Bird. . . .

What does Raphael, what do all the archangels, angels, seraphim, cherubim, principalities, dominions and powers, what do all the gazing fowls, think of our Klemm two-seater, so bravely soaring the heavens with golden wings outspread? One supposes them used to it by now; it is not a phœnix, not a strayed archangel, but just one among a flight of those great noisy birds that now disturb heaven's peace.

But to us it is a dream come true; never a man, woman, or child down all the ages but has dreamed of thus soaring and winging it through space, has conceived and desired what Bishop Wilkins called such volant automata. Though, as he said, the common desire has always been for wings fastened immediately to the body. That was Dædalus his manner; indeed, says the Bishop, it has been frequently attempted, not without some success. There was the English monk, Elmerus, about the Confessor's time, who did by such wings fly from a tower about a furlong; and so another from St. Mark's steeple in Venice; and Busbequius speaks of a Turk in Constantinople who attempted something this way. Mr. Burton doth believe that some new-fangled wit ('tis his cynical phrase) will some time or other find out this art. Though the truth is, most of these artists did unfortunately miscarry by falling down, and breaking their arms or legs, yet this may be imputed to their want of experience, and too much fear, which must needs possess men in such dangerous and strange attempts. Those things that seem very difficult and fearful at the first may grow very facile after frequent trial and exercise. And therefore he that would effect anything in this kind must be brought up to the constant practice of it from his youth, trying first only to use his wings in running on the ground, as an ostrich or tame geese will do, touching the earth with his toes; and so by degrees learn to rise higher, till he shall attain unto skill and confidence. . . .

And so much for flying like a bird, with wings attached to the body. But the mathematical Bishop preferred a flying chariot, which seemed to him altogether as probable and much more useful. It would be serviceable, said he, both for making discoveries in the Lunary World, and for the conveyance of a man to any remote place of this earth: as suppose to the Indies or Antipodes. How right he was!

Pull the stick towards you, calls the pilot (for there is a second stick in my cockpit, which I am now and then allowed to manipulate).

I pull, very gently; up goes our nose, seeking heaven.

Now push it from you.

We point earthward; it is like riding a bucking horse, his head and his heels up by turns. Then sideways; we bank, and all the chequered face of earth tilts up, now left, now right.

Now, says the pilot, we shall side-slip.

We move crabwise, leftward, more steeply than before, towards earth. So this is a side-slip, of which one has always heard. It is definitely agreeable.

We are now only about three hundred feet up, nearing the aerodrome, facing into wind. We nose down, drift slowly over a hedge. Green pastures rush up at us; the earthly sense of speed returns; we land at forty. The wheels touch ground; the stick is pulled back, bringing the tail to earth, dragging us to a standstill after a seventy-five yards' run. We taxy back to the hangar.

Climbing out, I look up and see dark birds with spread wings zooming between earth and heaven. Was I too there? Did I so soar, sail between worlds and worlds, winnow the buxom air, gazed by terrestrial eyes?

It is a pity that one feels after it a negligible but a just noticeable trifle of giddiness. Do the fowls of the air also so? It is said that some fishes are sea-sick, even after all these æons. . . .

Still, enormous bliss.

FOLLOWING THE FASHION

FOLLOWING THE FASHION

I HAVE a dress with puffed sleeves; the skirt is very long and full; about ten yards of silk, I think it took. It hangs in the wardrobe, taking a lot of room, because of the sleeves.

I have shoes with high heels; about three inches, I dare say. I can wear them if I want to.

I think I shall change my Morris, and get a small stream-lined green thing, and look smarter in the streets. It will not be so good for touring, but it will look better.

I may paint my nails red; or green, if that is coming in.

I shall write my memoirs, I think. I shall bring in every one I know, and have an index, so they can find themselves and their friends. There are plenty of things I can say about them. If they do not like it, they can lump it. It will serve them right, for having met me.

I may write a book about contemporary writers, too. They won't like that either, the things I shall say about them.

I can write tough-guy stories. What I mean is, I can write stories like this:

She was a grand girl. You're drunk, she said. But I

wasn't so drunk, either. I mean, I'd had a few, but I could see straight; and I could hold the wheel. I had the headlights on, too. To hell with those lamps, she said, and switched them down. Do you want to dazzle everything on the road, she said, so it rushes into us? You're nuts.

She was a grand girl. You're a grand girl, I said, and I switched on the big lamps again, and I held her waist with my left, and hugged her up to me close, so as I felt her warmth. That's the style, I said, and I saw the needle get up to sixty. Oh, you're crackers, she said. Driving like hell with the big lamps on and necking me with one arm. How to-night'll end, she said, I don't know. I really don't, do you? Like most nights end, I guess, said I, and that's when comes the dawn. Aw, you're crazy, said she. I told mother I'd be in by four. Well, you won't be in by four; maybe by eight. That's time enough for breakfast, isn't it? I know a swell place down the river. Oh, for heaven's sake, said she; we shall never get any place at this rate. And what must she do but start grabbing at the wheel, crying out I was all over the road. And so we were, after she started grabbing. Then she screamed out, and something hit us and we slewed right round.

There was the hell of a mess on the road. One of those little Austins, it was, and all crumpled up, and a man and a girl all crumpled up too. There was blood and glass and things around. But my Buick had only buckled a wing.

See here, I said, we can't do a thing. We'd best get on. She was being sick in the road; the blood had turned her up, I think. That and the shock. And seeing those two.

Here, I said, come on out of this. We can't do a thing. I put her in the Buick, and slewed around again and drove off. There was something banging loose, and I got out to look; it was the number plate, so I wrenched it off and took it inside. We didn't have the headlamps on now; the off one was smashed, anyway, by that bloody little Austin. I drove away. The steering was a bit funny, too. She never stopped crying and talking, it made me tired. Women can't get this: when a thing's done it's done. That's a thing no woman can ever get. They can't let it be. Hell, did I want that bloody little car to muscle into us that way? Aw, forget it.

All the time as I drive I seem to hear that damned radio saying, in its polite Oxford-Cambridge voice, "Before the news, there is a police message. Between two and three on Sunday morning an Austin seven car came into collision with another car, which apparently failed to stop. . . ." Failed nothing. I did stop, see? I stopped, and saw there wasn't a thing I could do, so I went on again.

Oh, to hell with your noise. . . .

Yes: I could write a story like that if I liked. Perhaps I will. Fine magazine stuff. What I mean is, a magazine would take it.

And I can write tough-guy poetry. A magazine would take that, too. I can write poetry like this (I call this one *To the Barricades*):

Mr. Jiggins goes to the circus.
(The girls, the hoops, the clowns, the seals, the hoop-
*   oes.)*
He has donned his Harrow tie,
But Borstal was his alma mater true.
He meets Mrs. Fortescue-Fox,
With a jade cigarette-holder, long and green like as-
*   paragus or a dead woman's fingers*
Or the pale weeds swaying in the duck-pond,
But never a sprig of rue.
You're so handsome, where you going?
Don't know where I'm going, where I am, where you
*   are, where the sweet hell anyone is.*
(Forward to the barricades! To the barricades—where
*   else?)*
Ohé! Ohé! mes brave petits! the fat is in the fire!
Εις τὸ πῦρ εκ τοῦ κᾰπνου.
As Lucian pointed out, things can always be worse.
Pink and stout he was, pranked out with rings and
*   gold chains, he was.*
What a fool he looked!
Dites donc, monsieur, si qu'on irait se coucher, n'est-ce
*   pas?*
Festinare nocet, tempore quæque suo qui facit, ille
*   sapit.*

In fact, no hurry.
(March, march, march, the feet of a thousand men
     marching as one. No hurry?)
They trample like artillery in my head.
Allons, allons, faites donner la garde!
But Mrs. Fortescue-Fox,
Unable to wait, flung herself upon the obdurate rocks.
Life is like that.
"But never mine," Mr. Jiggins cried.
And up washed the running tide,
Flowing up, casting corpses on the slimy beach,
Casting statues, casting coins, casting mermen and
     mermaids and old bowler hats.
Ting-a-ling-a-ling ring the bells of hell; where you
     bound now?
Allons, companions, we march to the barricades.

In the grey dawn of yesterday
We wipe away all tears:—perhaps.

There's another I call *Petrol Pumps*. But that's longer, and I won't print it here. It's fine magazine stuff too.

I like being in the fashion.

I may join the Communists.

Or I may write a novel a million words long, and very strong; the longest and strongest novel of the season.

The trouble about the fashions is, there are too

many going on at once, and you can't follow them all.

Sometimes I think I will give them all up, and just be dowdy.

FRATERNAL

.

FRATERNAL

IN HOW gentle and civilised an adult group we sit about the room! We talk, we read, we listen, we discuss, argue, contradict; but we are polite, considerate, forbearing: we behave, on the whole, grown-up. At meals, we pass things about; we help one another to food; we do not care who gets the most. We listen to one another's stories; we respect (within limits, and with considerable dissension) one another's opinions; we admire one another's several experiences and lives. We are assembled from far places; behind one of us is a background of hot Indian plains and rice swamps, of prowling snakes and tigers, of rice-devouring brown men. Behind another, prairies roll, skis and sledges glide over snow-bound plains, pine-clad mountains guard great lakes, moose and coyotes and gophers leap. Each trails behind him or her the clouds of a separate environment, a strange and different life.

You pass me honey: you do not watch how much of it I shall take. For all you observe, I may take it all, and there will be none left for any one else. Time was when you would have said, "That is too much; leave some for the rest of us." Time was when we should have eyed one another's plates with the zealous justice of the savage, feeling that good things should be apportioned in equal shares; we approved Miss Edgeworth's Frank, bidden by his papa to divide the sugared cake into equal parts and weigh them with scales.

The years roll back: a curtain lifts. I am no more in a drawing-room among adult beings having tea. I am seated at a table, among my savage kind; a nurse presides, feeding us with bread and butter. One eats the crumb; one arranges the bitten crusts in a circle under one's saucer, out, so one hopes, of sight. One tilts one's chair back on its hind legs, rocking to and fro.

"Now then, Miss R., don't tilt your chair."

"But A. is tilting his. May A. tilt his chair?"

Telling tales. We do not tell tales of one another now. . . .

Some one is licking the treacle from her bread.

"Now then, Miss J., that's not pretty. How often have I told you? . . . *Master W.!*"

Master W., in mood of ill-timed levity, has flung his bread and treacle at the ceiling. To our delight, it sticks there for a moment, before falling down. It leaves on the ceiling a sticky golden-brown smudge. Master W. is in trouble.

What undignified, what compromising situations have I seen you all in, brothers and sisters! Suspended head downwards by the knees from trees, like monkeys by their tails; rolling like barrels down green slopes to lie at the bottom and vomit; crawling along the top of a high wall to inhale the drain-trap placed (surely oddly) thereon; sitting astride on an overturned canoe at sea; slithering bare-legged up and down a rope; prone in impassioned sobbing on the floor; rolling over and over in angry wrestling; pulling hair, pinching, fisticuffing, hiding books under chair-cushions, as a dog buries bones, that no other may have a turn of them. You, sitting reading there with your pipe, I remember your seizing my book and flinging it out of the window, that I might desist from reading. You, who do not smoke, I remember how you and I took the cigar tops cut off by uncles and smoked them; how we all trooped to the village toy-shop and bought Woodbines, and smoked them sitting in a row on the pig-sty roof. I could repeat the precise order in which we each met defeat at this pastime and retired. Yes: I remember all of you in the most ridiculous positions. . . .

We cannot hide from one another: we know too much. We know one another's faults, virtues, catastrophes, mortifications, triumphs, rivalries, desires, and how long we can each hang by our hands to a bar. We have been banded together under pack codes and tribal laws. The remembered jungle is behind us, with its pleasures and pains, its follies, adventures and jests.

Jests: yes. We share a comic background, that could never be explained to others. A chance word may touch a spring set deep in the common stock of memory, and loose on us a joke, a surge of laughter, that is out of all proportion to the word uttered, for it rises from those deeps where forgotten and remembered jokes lie tangled in a giggling past. Giggling is the word for the excessive, the uncontrollable mirth that shook us when young, that shakes us even now when together, and to which no other has the clue.

Contradiction is moderated. Argument, which still rages on every topic, political, theological, literary, sociological, factual, has grown more complex; it no longer tails off into the bald competition in endurance of "it is," "it isn't," "it is," "it isn't," "it is." Activity has dwindled: no more do we sally forth to climb roofs or trees. Manners have improved: no more do we track passers-by along the street in furtive detective-formation, registering clues in hissing whispers as we go. We behave civilised, even when in a pack. But pack jokes remain. They may be no better than other jokes; they are often worse. But they are jokes by themselves, and are among the marks which distinguish the pleasures of fraternal association from any other.

GETTING RID

GETTING RID

LIFE is one long struggle to disinter oneself, to keep one's head above the accumulations, the ever-deepening layers of objects, of litter (for so I call those objects which I do not want), which attempt to cover one over, steadily, almost irresistibly, like falling snow. The danger is (one has heard) that one is lulled to sleep beneath the drifts, and will not (so also one has heard) wake again, but lie for ever besnowed, buried, unable to stir. Courage, then: fight the insidious, the deadly drifts while there is yet time; up and scatter them to the winds, tear them to shreds, fling them into dustbins, into the street, anywhere, and stand up free and disencumbered to abide the next storms.

If one had the wisdom to cast out litter as it arrives each day, one would not have these mighty periodic disencumberments; one would live more easily; but one would miss that tremendous, that spacious, sense of easement which follows a great clearance.

Tear them up, then, those piles of letters which you have never answered, nor will. Are you not born free? Shall anyone with a pen or a typewriter, a stamp or two, and some stationery, have the power to assault you, to bully you, to tear your precious time and your frail brain and attention, so sorely needed else-

where, to shreds by making you answer his letters?
You do not, I am sure, write to all and sundry asking
them this and that, requesting them for time, for gifts,
for attention to some business in which you, but not
they, may chance to be interested: you give them
credit for having their own interests, their own work,
their own lives and schemes. You let them, in fact (I
hope), alone. But how unusual this abstention appears to be! Letters arrive for you; pamphlets, newspaper cuttings, books, discursive remarks, all manner
of suggestions and requests. There they lie, reproachful piles, awaiting your attention.

If only you had a secretary. . . . But I take it that,
like most of us, you have not a secretary. Even if
you had, you would, I suppose, have to give her some
indication of how you wished her to deal with the
manifold topics opened up by your correspondents.
But you have not even a secretary. You would, should
you attempt to cope with the situation, have to find
stationery, stamps, words, forms of courteous refusal,
idle chat, turn off from your typewriter the paper
which waits those laborious stampings and stammerings
which it is your profession or your pleasure to make
on it, and with which you are already so far behind
time, and replace it by one piece of notepaper after
another, on which you imprint the date (if you can
call it to mind) and the disgusting word "Dear," and
then pause to collect the kind of words apt to the
distracting occasion. By the time you have done all
this, your somewhat weak (it is probably somewhat

weak) intellect will be all-to scattered and depraved, and you will find it hard to turn it again on to its proper tasks. Imagination, after its efforts to find words of polite and idiotic refusal, thanks, and regrets, will lie down fatigued, and boggle when set at its customary courses. You will have to give it a rest, and take the car out instead.

No; you were better not to tackle those piles. Let them lie and grow. But, one day when the reproach of the great unanswered becomes too heavy a burden, or when your groaning writing-table is so deep ensnowed that it holds no room for anything you may desire to keep on it on your own account, then rise up, either calmly or in noble rage, and destroy. Shovel the litter into some deep bin; let the scavengers, those kindly, cocked-hatted men, carry it hence, to the great pits and furnaces which shall receive it, and transmute it into the rags whence it came. Eternal process of to-ing and fro-ing, from rags to paper, from paper to rags: whether is the worse condition? A few minutes ago you would have said paper. But now, having rid yourself of papers, you turn, strong and collected, in calm of mind all passion spent, to deal with rags.

Rags! How these encumber cupboards and drawers, hanging on hooks and on pegs, relics of earlier ages, which to be seen abroad in now were very shame, even if they were not so riddled and devoured by those gluttonous lepidoptera who make your cupboards their home. On most occasions, no doubt, you are wearily acquiescent in this; one look at the cupboards or drawers, and you turn away back to more normal and congenial employs. And quite right, too.

Neglected heaps we in by-corners lay,
Where they become to worms and moths a prey,
Forgot, in dust and cobwebs let them rest,
While we return to where we first digrest.

But, now, heartened and strengthened by your victory over the papers, you face the rags, you fling them out, you decide that no claim of old affection or habit shall induce you to wear them again, to clean, to mend or to tolerate them. And, as for leaving them where they are, is it your duty to feed that tribe of greedy stolephage insects who have come unbidden to your table? Experience throughout the ages has shown that you may safely leave that to their Creator. Remove, then, their food; brush and shake it; tie it up in bundles; it is for the Poor. If the Poor reject it, as well they may, it can return to the transmuting furnace and boilers, there to be encharted once again. One day you may be throwing it into your wastepaper basket; and hanging in your cupboards for the moths those letters which you have just now so triumphantly flung for a while out of your life.

This getting rid is a kind of intoxication; be wary lest it carry you too far. Do not lay rash hands on all the letters, all the journals, all the garments, that you see lying about. You may want some of them again. Exercise moderation in destruction, that heady lust.

And when you have finished, you will sit down, happy, victorious and rid, while the enemy creeps on again, seeping in through every crevice, surrounding and submerging you with relentless, unpausing advance. Your pleasure in victory is brief, and haunted by the imminence of future defeats. For riddable litter comes on like the sea, and there is no staying it. Even in prison cells, they say, litter enters and must daily be removed. It is our mortal heritage, and a losing war against nature that we wage.

But, for the moment, those letters, those newspapers, are gone. Thus far, we are, for the moment, one up on nature, that sinister, wily, and determined harridan, against whom civilisation wars perpetually and, for the most part, in vain.

HATCHING EGGS

HATCHING EGGS

ACTUALLY, I do not know that hatching is the right word, for I never, by human warmth, delivered any chicken from its shell. Neither would "sitting on" be correct, for that was not the method adopted. I suppose incubating is the word. Anyhow, the pleasure lay in hope and dreams, never in consummation. We carried our eggs on the person by day, under the pillow by night. Only one at a time, and when it broke we began on another. They were mostly laid by hens, but once I found a duck's egg in the road, huge and pale green. How far it might already be advanced towards the duckling stage, I had no means of knowing; but I adopted it forthwith and stowed it away in the front of my sailor frock, the largest and proudest of the eggs on the persons of a family at the moment a prey to acute eggomania. There it lay, in that repository designed by heaven for carrying about oranges, books, rabbits, and kittens, so that the wearing of sailor suits, male and female, made a family inclined to thinness bulge in front as if they had been reared on some rich health food. My egg lay, I think, alone, and hand-kerchief enwrapped; when tree or rock climbing was indulged in, it was removed and carefully laid in some snug cache.

For how many days I nursed this greenish and pregnant treasure, this shrine of a fluffy golden being who should emerge in the fullness of time, who should owe its happy waddling life to me, I know not. They were glorious days, if few. I walked and gingerly ran, dream-wrapped; I was with duckling, and must walk warily. When in the slippery paths of youth with heedless steps I ran, the bouncing against my bosom of my duck-to-be recalled me to the cautiousness of prospective motherhood.

How I would love it! It would be my dandling, my nestlechick, my pet. With my own hands I would teach it to swim, to run, to jump (for we were accustomed to organise hurdle races for our pets, of whatever species). Mine would be the swiftest duck e'er entered for the stakes. It would accompany me everywhere, sitting on my lap at meals, at lessons, bathing with me in the sea. How, too, it would love me! Why does the duckling love her so, people would ask, as of Mary's lamb. Well, she loves the duck, you see, they would reply. And was I not giving it life, tending it, sacrificing for it other pleasures? Should it not, when it came to perception, gratefully quack, with Joseph Addison,

> *Unnumber'd comforts to my soul*
> *Thy tender care bestow'd,*
> *Before my infant heart conceived*
> *From whom those comforts flow'd?*

Thus I mused in my maternal meditations, moving delicately about house, shore, road, hill-side, my hands often crossed over my breast as in some holy picture. I felt safe, guarded, protected, with my dear and perilous burden; a thousand liveried angels lackeyed me, and I knew that this time a duck would be born. I would often take out the egg and put my ear to it as to a shell, to listen for faint cheepings, which I sometimes fancied that I heard. I wondered what would happen if it should hatch by night, beneath my pillow. . . . Suppose that I were to wake one morning and find a smothered duckling, whose cries had failed to wake me? But we had been told that chickens and ducklings usually hatched by day, so this chance seemed remote.

The end came, as usual. The liveried angels went off duty, and with heedless steps I ran across the slippery stone floor of a room, and fell prone on my chest. A horrid smash, and my pet flowed away, sticky, addled, smelling of the corruption of all mortality, and past return were all its dandled days.

In the ensuing mess and bitterness of baulked hope, my one and chilly comfort was that there had never, it seemed, been duck life in that shell. I had not been with duckling, only with egg; and with stale and ancient egg of date incalculable. My nestlechick had been but a fluffy golden vision, conceived in the pregnant rovings of my brain, never by duck and drake in sweet communion linked. It had been the child of my doting dreams alone. But, while they lasted, what doting and what dreams!

HERESIES

HERESIES

I KNOW how the great heretics felt; I can enter into their fervorous assertions, their obstinate denials, their ingenious and fantastic inventions, their wild day-dreams concerning the world, the heavens and themselves. I can share their triumphant firmness in error, which would keep them ergotising sleepless through days and nights, frapling one against another, pro and con, across some seeming-small but bridgeless gulf which yawned between them and their opponents; I know the proud self-confidence which, after all these eager ergotisms, so often sent them heaven or hellward encharioted in flames.

More, when I recall some of those peculiar heresies which have down the ages made men and women feel so strongly, argue so fiercely, slay and die with such a ruthless calm, I feel in myself a responsive pleasure in nearly all. There must have been something in these strange delusions, I tell myself, that they inspired such confidence. Indeed, they have a quality of persistence which discovers them to be deeply rooted in human nature; scarce one in past centuries that you will not find echoed to-day; scarce one which I do not find re-hereticised in my own soul, at one moment or another, for the soul has its days and moods.

I am often pleased, for instance, to be an Origenist, as have been so many amiable men, and to think that there shall be no man damned, but all saved at the last, including the Devil himself. There are moments when I like to be Eustathian, to look on marriage as sinful, and wish, with Sir Thomas Browne, that there were some more delicate way to populate the world; other moments when polygamy captivates me, and I desire, with the Anabaptists and Mormons, that everyone should wed to the top of his bent. On hot days in the south I am Adamite, and wish to stroll abroad clad only in what Jeremy Taylor called rustick impudence; when skies are cold and sad I turn Manichee and hate the flesh. Often I am Pelagian, and vainly talk against original sin, boasting the potency of man's will to virtue; or I embrace Arianism, Socinianism or Photinianism, defying Athanasian thunders. How frequently am I one with the Fraticelli, their partiality to not too monotonous affections, their distaste for manual labour; or the Dulcinists, who combined with these errors the repugnance felt by the Waldensians for the clergy, for the cult of the saints, for the rights of property, and for the indissolubility of marriage.

Often too, I belong to the Agonyclites, and will not kneel; I like to be Collyridian, Messalian, Quartodeciman, semi-Pelagian, in turn; I will even experiment in Partial-Diluvianism, and maintain that the Flood left parts of the earth's surface uncovered; I will participate in a hundred of those enthusiastic and fanatical errors which are a heritage from our audacious, speculating and so wrong-headed fathers.

These damnable and damnèd tenets are charming to hold, these poisoned streams sweet to the palate. That humanity, so imperilled by hereticide, so close to ravening lion and crackling flame, could be so ingenious and so determined in straying from the true path, is not strange to him who peruses human history. That Montanist and Donatist, flung into the same arena by Emperors to encounter hungry Christianophagous animals, should turn their backs on one another with expressions of distaste and advance into the jaws of different lions, resolved not even to be joined in martyrdom, is natural enough to him who is familiar with odium theologicum. For heretics too, have their portion in the heritage of this great odium; while in the grip of one heresy I condemn and abominate the others as if I were a partridge in a cage. (*Like as a partridge taken and kept in a cage, so is the heart of the proud.* Ecclesiasticus xi. 30.)

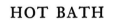

HOT BATH

HOT BATH

A HOT bath! I cry, as I sit down in it; and again, as I
lie flat, a hot bath! How exquisite a vespertine pleasure,
how luxurious, fervid and flagrant a consolation for
the rigours, the austerities, the renunciations of the
day. All day I have moved about in chill air, in fog,
in bitter and annihilating blasts, in inclement elements
for which the tender human frame, contrived for the
balmy airs of Eden, was never made. I have sat upright in a chair and tapped with stiff fingers on a
typewriter; I have wrung numb thoughts and words
out of a frozen brain, transmitting them on to paper
in a gellid trickle; I have walked through chill murk
and contagious fogs, with sore eyes and throat, every
breath a pain, the grime of a great ennebuled city
choking pores and lungs, the mazed world a darkness
and a doubt, the round red sun extinguished, quite
put out. I have, in brief, suffered angry winter's chid-
ing tongue and dark brief day.

And now the bath; and now hot water gushing lav-
ishly from a chromium tap into a white porcelain bed,
spreading thin and clear, then verdurously bubbling
round green and piney bath salts, assuming the tinge
of a glasshouse full of ferns, or of tropical forests.
Soaked in green light, with two small red ducks bob-

bing about me, I lie at ease, frayed nerves relaxed, numbed blood running round again on its appointed, circular mortal race, frozen brain melting, thawing, expanding into a strange exotic efflorescence in this warm pine forest. Bare winter suddenly is changed to spring,

> *And on old Hiems' thin and icy crown*
> *An odorous chaplet of sweet summer buds*
> *Is, as in mockery, set. . . .*

Like those Japanese paper flowers which gently unfold and bloom in bowls of water, thoughts and dreams burgeon, the mind puts out boughs and sprigs of blossom and ripe fruits, inebriating and enticing the charmed soul. Music seems to sound: is it that music of the spheres which only (so we are told) the chaste ear hears, or is it some strayed mermaid? Or does the dandled brain itself dream harmony, drowned in warm sweetness like a tropicked ship? The waters lap gently about the almost submerged island; sirens sing, the lotus flower opens, naiads move in rhythm, genius flows like wine, poems, tales and pictures create themselves, swim in heavenly brightness, and dissolve. I am in the Golden Age; in Paradise; in the Fortunate Isles; in the gardens of the Hesperides and of Alcinous; in the floating gardens of Montezuma. I lie in Eden's bower, among odorous gums and balsams, or in a lake that to the fringed bank with myrtle crowned her crystal mirror holds, while universal Pan, knit with the

Graces and the hours in dance, leads on the eternal spring. So, lulled in these flowers with dances and delight, I drowse entranced.

The Emperor Commodus is reported to have had a hot bath seven times a day; and who can blame him? Rich women have bathed themselves in milk, sometimes in the milk of five hundred she-asses at once. But water is better, for milk, if hot, would form a skin. The slimy touch of that white, crinkly skin on one's own . . . but perhaps the rich women's slaves kept the milk bath in continual motion, so that no skin could form. Fear of skin must have been the shadow that hung over those rich women's baths. The shadow that hangs over mine is the fear of cooler water, dread lest the hot delight running from the taps should grow temperate, tepid, neither hot nor cold, to be spewed out of the mouth. That will be the end: it is already the end: the warm bower cools, its flowers fade, its songs die; the water, which I ruffle and splash to warm it, chills moment by moment.

Still I sojourn here, alone and palely loitering, though the sedge is withered from the lake and no birds sing. For I sent the bath towel to the wash this morning, and omitted to put out another. I have no towel.

IGNORANCE

IGNORANCE

1. *Of one's neighbours*

No, I do not know the names of anyone in this street, these flats, this square. No, I do not know who Mrs. Miller is, or where she lives. This flat is my flat, and quite self-contained; I do not know my neighbours. Pride and self-containment swell me; I keep myself to myself, and wish you to know it. Who and what is this Mrs. Miller, that you should suppose I know of her? Has Mrs. Miller the run of my home, or I of Mrs. Miller's? The savage pride of the cave-dweller surges in me. No, I know nothing about any of the other caves, thank you. Their inhabitants are probably despicably uncivilised, and, for all I know, keep parrots. You will have to find out their names for yourself.

What? Something has happened at Mrs. Miller's? There has been a burglary, a murder, a fire? The police are here, and do not know which door to break down? Alas, it is too late for me to be concerned with that now; you should have told me at once. How can I now conduct you to Mrs. Miller's door and share in the fun? You must ask someone else, and next time you ask me anything, kindly state your reason first.

2. Of *current literature*

No, I am afraid I have not read that either. It is good, you say? I am sure you are right. But I have no time for all these novels and things. I cannot imagine how you make time for them. You find they are worth it? They do not *look* good. Not that I see them; but they do not sound good, from the advertisements and reviews. Not that I read advertisements and reviews. I like to keep myself clear from all this second-rate stuff. Am I not afraid of missing something good? Well, I feel that the danger of reading something bad outweighs that risk. Yes, as you point out, I contribute to current literature myself. But then I scarcely *read* my own stuff, after all. And the point is, I get money for writing it. If anyone gave me money for reading, that would be another matter.

Yes, I am going off on Monday for a month in the country. You were going to give me some of your review copies, did you say? But now you will sell them instead. . . . Oh, well . . .

3. Of *gossip*

They have quarrelled? No, I had not heard. I never hear about people's quarrels. And Daphnis and Chloe are to divorce? I had not heard that either. You hear all these news; I do not. No one tells me; I am too busy to inquire. It is better not to know; it avoids embarrassing moments. When I meet people, there is no subject I need to avoid; I can say anything. It is better so. It would be so tiresome not being able to mention Phyllis to Chloe, or Corydon to Daphnis, just because there are entanglements. After all, is not all life one long entanglement, and is it worth while to inform oneself about every knot? It is so much simpler not to know. And such things are not really interesting. Human beings being what they are, affections, animosities, meetings, partings, intimacies, estrangements, libel actions, occur all the time; to keep *au fait* with them would tax the most alert mind and take all one's time. As for me, I am happiest among my books.

You are going? But I thought you had something to tell me. . . .

4. *Of wickedness*

Can you understand wanting to act like that? I must say that I cannot. What I mean is, I am no saint, heaven knows, and I have my faults as much as anyone, but when it comes to things like that, one simply cannot enter into them. For instance, I can lose my temper, and say hasty things, but when it comes to real delight in cruelty, such as Nero's, or Caligula's, or the Nazis', or our ancestors', I simply cannot begin to understand it. Nor wanting to make marks in other people's books. Nor taking books and not returning them. Nor stealing stockings. And all this pornography one hears of. It never comes my way. One hears of books, of films, of postcards, of pictures, but I never see any. No doubt I am very ignorant. Bishops seem always to contrive to see improper films. They must have an excellent information service; of course, bishops cannot afford to be ignorant. What a time they must have!

But I see you think me a prig. That is the worst of ignorance; people either think you stupid or a prig. Probably both.

5. *Of one's pass-book*

This, I presume, is my pass-book, returned by the bank after being made up. I shall not open it; I shall put it away in a drawer as it is. It is one of those many books which are better unread. Am I Pandora, to open an odious box and set cares flying loose to sting me? Why should I depress myself by looking at all those figures, and the ridiculous sum they write in pencil at the end? I suppose they will tell me when they do not care to cash my cheques any more, and until then I shall go on drawing them, and shall not brood. The Bible tells us not to worry, but to take no thought for the morrow. If I were to begin poring over my pass-book (I cannot imagine why my bank should always give it a capital P and B, as if it were so desperately important) I should be paralysed, I could not live at all. Every mouthful would choke me; I could not so much as buy the means of subsistence, such as National Benzole or Shell, without hesitation and pain. While as for a wash and polish for my car, or a shampoo and set for my hair, I should cut them out altogether. And go nowhere, and see no one. I have anguish enough already at quarter days, what with rent and gas and electricity and telephone and bills, and that insolent income tax twice a year. If I were to read and remember my pass-book, it would be worse still. . . .

So I do not read it. I walk in trust, hoping that I am still well on the hither side of indigence, and that my estate will prosperously endure. I spend, I consume, I commune with the angels, I live, I turn to rude facts a genteel and well-bred back.

The day will come. My landlord, the Gas Light & Coke Company, the Borough Council Electricity Department, the Controller of the London Telephone Service, the Income Tax Inspector, the very milkman, will all one day receive back from their banks cheques marked R.D. I shall be run down, run out of my estate, finished. However then I may strive after Ignorance, that tranquil maid, I shall not be permitted to dwell with her again. Perhaps, if I were to open and read this sealed book now . . .

> *Yet ah! why should I know my fate,*
> *Since sorrow never comes too late,*
> *And happiness too swiftly flies?*
> *Thought would deny my paradise*
> *No more! Where ignorance is bliss . . .*

Enough. Return the thing to its drawer.

IMPROVING THE DICTIONARY

IMPROVING THE DICTIONARY

ON A blank page at the beginning of the Supplementary Volume of my Dictionary, I record emendations, corrections, additions, earlier uses of words, as I come on them in reading. Ah, I say, congratulating myself, here Messrs. Murray, Bradley, Craigie and Onions are nearly a century out; here were sailors, travellers and philosophers chattering of sea turtles from the fifteen-sixties on, and the Dictionary will not have them before the sixteen-fifties. And how late they are with estancias, iguanas, anthropophagi, maize, cochineal, canoes, troglodytes, cannibals and hammocks. As to aniles, or old wives' tales, they will not let us have this excellent noun at all.

Thus I say to myself, as I enter my words and dates. To amend so great a work gives me pleasure; I feel myself one of its architects; I am Sir James Murray, Dr. Bradley, Sir William Craigie, Dr. Onions, I belong to the Philological Society; I have delusions of grandeur. Had I but world enough and time, I would find earlier uses of all the half million words, I would publish another supplement of my own, I would achieve at last my early ambition to be a lexicographer.

If there is a drawback to this pure pleasure of doing good to a dictionary, I have not yet found it. Except that, naturally, it takes time.

LISTENING IN

LISTENING IN

WHO would have thought it? I press a switch, and my room is full of the clamour of voices from strange worlds, a thousand fantasies of calling shapes and airy tongues, on sands and shores and desert wildernesses, that may startle well but not astound the virtuous mind. . . . The coconut harvest is gathered in Malaya; tobacco is planted in Nyasaland, tea in Ceylon, timber hauled in Oregon, ship-loads of daffodils languish on Scilly quays while high seas rage, herds of reindeer trek across Canadian snows, and hearty voices from America strive to greet us above the rushing noises of the severing Atlantic. Or small, flat, twanging voices sound, telling us about Art, about Architecture, about Currency, crossing the "t" in often, dotting the "i" in opposite, speaking of *de*fects, figyures, ideels, currencee, dwelling fondly on those shy syllables in English words which are meant to be seen and not heard, and are only put in to make spelling more difficult. Or Youth prophesies in sad tones that the future will be quite different from the past, Eskimos sit naked in their igloos and spear whales in Hudson's Strait, and the sky parades before us its marching regiments of planets and of stars. Had I time, I should listen to all of it, and know, very soon, everything, even the prices of fat cattle.

Then the music. How delicious to sit at ease and hear, without visible orchestra, this harmony that rains upon the ear. It might be, it very possibly is, that heavenly symphony, that music of the spheres to which Pythagoras used to say that the celestial universe revolved in tune, unheard by practically every man but him, for none but he was pure enough. Plato added sirens to the orchestra, seating one of these on each celestial orb and causing her to sing, so that at the honey-sweet chorus gods and men marvelled. It must certainly be so, said Milton, endorsing this delightful celestial concert, for the spheres would have long since wearied of their rotatory labours, had they not had music to sustain and encourage them. Other poets support this.

> *The turning vault of heaven formèd was,*
> *Whose starry wheeles he hath so made to passe,*
> *As that their movings do a musicke frame,*
> *And they themselves still daunce unto the same.*

The lark can hear this music, the nightingale too, and so should we, but for our grossness. It is

> *the heavenly tune, which none can hear*
> *Of human mould with grosse unpurged ear.*

Milton blames Prometheus, who robbed us of our innocence; others have put it down more to the error of our first parents, who are said to have been, until they fell, so tele-visionary and tele-audient that they could both see and hear the farthest, faintest star. Anyhow, and for whatever cause, we are now too sunk in brutishness to hear these heavenly harmonies. If our souls were pure, chaste, and snow-white, as was formerly that of Pythagoras, then should we hear that lovely rumour of the circling stars; or so they all say.

But what? Do I not hear the very sound? Does it not steal in ravishment upon my ear? What other than the rotating spheres and their melodious sirens can make these unseen harmonies? Have I indeed won the reward of a blameless life and become, like Pythagoras before me (and a few birds), celestially audient, cœlo-tuned? So, indeed, it seems.

> *So dear to Heav'n is Saintly chastity*
> *That when a soul is found sincerely so,*
> *A thousand liveried Angels lacky her . . .*
> *And in cleer dream and solemn vision*
> *Tell her of things that no gross ear can hear.*

This must be what is occurring to me. How gratifying; how delightful. How Plato's Er would have envied me: he only speculated on the spheral music; he never heard a note of it. Perhaps one evening I shall hear a bat squeak. Meanwhile the celestial orchestra performs for me.

> *then listen I*
> *To the celestial* Sirens *harmony,*
> *That sit upon the nine enfolded Sphears. . . .*

But what is this? What shriek tears the soft air to quivering shreds? Heaven, who has given me such signal favours, protect me now, for a soprano has broken loose upon the divine orchestra, and her savage cry rends the evening peace as if a cat shrieked upon a roof. This is no siren, but rather some Fury, busy about her barbarous and vengeful tasks. So shrieked the Erinnyes, pursuing Orestes for his unnatural crimes, so the Harpies, gobbling the food of poor Phineus as they flew down black winds.

A soprano! What terrific cataclysm of nature gave tongue in such sort, what shrill and squawking bird was slain long since by huntsman, so that the race of men were condemned to have among them for ever its voice in human female shape? Procne remetamorphosed, and returning from her chelidonian adventures with more than chelidonian voice wherewith to plague Tereus and all mankind for their sins. That singing sea-maid on a dolphin's back to whom Oberon listened from his rocky promontory, and to hear whom certain stars shot madly from their spheres, sang, it is sure, in a sweet contralto, smooth and shadow-haunted and creaming as the long run of waves into a deep green gully, or the humming of summer winds in a pine wood. Not a star would have deserted its own rotatory and siren music for a soprano. It fills the air with barbarous dissonance: but only for a moment. A touch, and it abruptly falls on silence. I turn a knob, and am in France; a cascade of sharp and throaty Gallic patters in my ears.

Who would have thought it?

But far be it from me to close on a note of pure content. Sopranos are all very well, and so are trombones and xylites and all such barbarous noises, for I can quickly rid myself of them. But not so with all airy abominations, for some of these are inserted out of due place, in the midst of news which I desire to hear. Such is the case with cricket. Cricket is, I understand, palatable news to some; they hang on bat and ball, on test match, ashes, and wicket; and, reading on news-posters in the street such catastrophic and momentous head-lines as "ENGLAND FALLS," their hearts fall too. Very good: I would not grudge them their news. There is, at the end of the News Bulletin, a section entitled Sport. It is in this section that the results of games played with balls are announced, and those who do not desire to hear these may switch off at the word "Sport." But too often cricket rises surging out of its place like a river in flood, breaking its levees, rushing out of Sport into the main news, so that, having heard about the weather, and settling down all agog for the odd tale of European events, I hear instead the odious word Cricket complacently uttered, and followed by a drab tale of balls flung and hit, runs run, inningses declared, and players in or out. And how can I switch off this dreary stuff, when I know not at what moment it will end and give place to news that I might want to hear?

I submit that this is not fair play, not (to use its own foolish phraseology) cricket. What I mean is, you might as well put the Italian-Abyssinian crisis in the Sport section. Better.

This must be mended. It is rousing up and down England an ugly feeling of resentment. We are a patient people, but our patience has limits, as our monarchs and other rulers have from time to time found. This business of misplacing the news items may be the rock on which the British Broadcasting Corporation will founder.

LOGOMACHY

LOGOMACHY

STRANGE! The quiet and sunlit garden, in which, but a moment since, we lay enwrapt in post-prandial dominical peace, affably exchanging sugared and drowsy comments on delphiniums, Marxism, Hitlerism, religion, literature, landscape, and life, has suddenly become a Whipsnade, noisy with the howls, snarls, chatterings, gibberings, trumpetings, roarings, yappings, of creatures who differ concerning words. Someone spoke of pornography—what more natural, what more inevitable, a topic, since it connects with Marxism, Hitlerism, religion, literature, landscape, life, and probably delphiniums? In brief, it connects, they say, with everything; someone had been sent a boot and shoe catalogue between whose lines it lay, or so it seemed to her, like *foie gras* between bread in sandwiches. Be that as it may, we spoke, still drowsy and still sugared, still post-prandial and still dominical, of pornography. And a very amicable course the conversion would doubtless have pursued on this congenial topic, but that we discovered that we did not agree as to the meaning of the term. Two schools of thought arose: one held that the word, if correctly used, must imply pleasure given, or intended to be given, to the readers of the pornographic narrative or discourse or what not; the other that the intentions of the writer were irrelevant, and that pornography was, quite simply, what the Greek word means, always provided that sufficient wealth of detail was supplied. The battle raged; one school accused the other of putting a gloss on the word, the other retaliated with charges of having an etymological mind, of pedantic insensitiveness to accepted shades of meaning. Other words broke in; we spoke of phenomenal, of litotes and meiosis, of the derivation of ilk (someone erroneously conceived it to come from the Latin *illic*), of anthropophagi (someone erroneously maintained that these should properly be human), of erotic, of melodrama, of prelate, presbyter, and priest, of highbrow, of a dozen more such contentious points. The garden rang again with our logomachy, with our loud ergoting pro and con. All were conceited, scornful, happy, crying ha-ha like the war-horse charging in battle. There is poetomachy, bibliomachy, angelomachy, theologomachy, gastromachy, erotomachy, a hundred other strifes; of them all, logomachy is the most absorbing, the most calculated to fill with sound and fury a pleasant Sunday afternoon.

But, during a moment's pause, I recollected how logomachs have been disapproved of, scornfully entreated, regarded as petty squabblers and unworthy quibblers, out of tune with the infinite, out of place on Parnassus. I recalled John Milton, how, in a Cambridge oration, he railed against logomachia. *Has argutiolas*, he coldly exclaimed, *inanes quæstiunculas;* these quibblings, these empty little questions. And, "It is abundantly clear how little these trifles lead to integrity of life and cultivated manners, which are the greatest good. This logomachia neither contributes to the general welfare, nor in any way to the honour and profit of our country. Two things most advance and ornament a country—fine speaking and brave action; but this litigious battling of discrepant opinion neither instructs in eloquence, inculcates prudence, nor incites to brave deeds."

And that, to be sure, is the main thing, is it not?

"Away, then," continued John Milton, "with these cunning chatterboxes. . . ."

He must have been right. Nevertheless, as the word-battle swells up around me, I cannot help thinking that it does, after all, incite to some eloquence.

MEALS OUT

MEALS OUT

1. *On the roof*

SHUT the attic skylight door; that is right. Do not let
us put our toes through such tiles as we can con-
veniently avoid; there was some trouble last time the
Brave Alpine Climber Band was on the roof. We will
encamp in the valley between the two smoking peaks
of Etna and Vesuvius. Here is the rucksack; it has
five oranges, seven rusks, three bottles of ginger pop,
twopence worth of pear drops, and a mug. And a
packet of Woodbines, in case we feel brave enough
for a smoke. Only no one must be sick on the roof;
it would be too disgusting. Anyone who means to be
sick must get through the skylight first, or else swarm
down the gutter pipe into the yard.

The B.A.C.B. is enjoying its well-earned meal. It
has climbed far to-day, and got very dirty and rather
scraped. Pass round the mug; bang in the glass stop-
pers of the pop bottles, and do not let too much run
fizzing over the roof. Turn and turn about; Climber
Nansen's turn is lasting too long. Have we finished?
All but the pear drops and the cigarettes. We will now
sit astride on that gable, or rather that mountain ridge,
and suck the former and smoke the latter.

A fine view indeed. The yard lies spread beneath us, and the stable and barn and outhouse roofs lift their peaks and gables around us. We see the kitchen door, and the kennel, and the wall that divides the yard from the fruit garden and the lawn. We can see right over this, and over the holly hedge into the lane and the great field that slopes down beyond it. We can see the fields even beyond that; the corn-field with the footpath running through it, and the reapers at work, the large elms that hide the lane to the village. The universe simmers before us in a hot August drone. We are drowsy in the sun. We have a pear-drop in one side of the mouth, a Woodbine in the other. We suck; we smoke. Climber Nansen pales, spews out his pear-drop, drops his Woodbine, reclines. You had better, Climber Nansen, get back through the skylight before it is too late. Crawl away quickly; quicker, can't you; I am crawling behind you; with me it is nearly already too late. All things are with God, but He must not permit anything to occur on the roof. . . .

2. *On the pavement*

The Café-Restauran Garcia has an orange and blue striped awning outside it, shading the pavement from the sun and the moon. Beneath it we sit at our table; we sit on, long after we have ceased to dine, drinking coffee, sipping cognac, eating lumps of sugar, smoking, talking, looking at the plaza with its elegant ordinations of palms, oranges and lemons, listening to the band which plays there. Mexican gentlemen and ladies stroll about, sit and drink at tables, twang musical instruments. It is balmy, it is warm, the night smells of lemon trees. There is a yellow ochre cathedral at the other side of the plaza, built by Spanish missionaries four centuries ago. The houses round the plaza are the houses of old Spain. Beyond them rise against the violet sky the dim serrated peaks of Mexican mountains. I eat oblongs of cane sugar, dipped in the cognac of my companion. Brandy-sugar: it sweetens and burns the blood, sets the night to a merry tune. The band has stopped, but the Mexican gentlemen still twang strings, and there is singing.

Hey, mozo! Otro aguardiente! Y mas azucar.

NEW YEAR'S EVE

NEW YEAR'S EVE

WALKING in the fields on the last of those brief, chill and gentle afternoons that run the old year out, I felt the cool damp air of Hampshire, sweet with fir and heather, stir about me like cold wings. The sky loomed greyly over the purple-brown line of the moor, but melted into blue squares and ovals over the western stubble-fields, and glinted above Farewell Hanger into a pool of gold. Crossing two stiles, I came to a foot-bridge; beneath it the full Rother gurgled with song. The earth squelched under foot; a thrush whistled in a dripping copse of holly and oak.

In the still, dreaming heart of the Hampshire winter, the year turned, and would be made new. So wild and deep a mystery as this stirred the naked woods, whispered in the cold brook, whistled flutily from the holly copse. Immemorial Christmas, the year's turn, the sun's birth, the earth's cold saturnalia, whereat soft-footed elves patter and chuckle and gobble and trip, shaking silver drops from the holly, sucking their teeth as they squelch in the mud of the small deep lanes and cow-trodden fields. There is small friendliness in the year's end: it is secret, cold, a prehistoric act played each twelvemonth by the drowsy primeval gods who have scarcely yet, after these few thousands of brief years, observed the intrusion of the fussy little creature strutting on two legs through their ancient habitations.

There was a sighing, soft and cold, as if the year turned over in his sleep.

Or as if the sky slid earthwards in a sheet of rain, which in fact at that moment occurred.

NOT GOING TO PARTIES

NOT GOING TO PARTIES

It is apparent which door the party is behind, for all down the street pours and swells its jocund rumour, as of Bacchus and his merry crew. It guides me to it, as the sweet church bells guide worshippers to prayer. Hark, hark, and yet again!

> *This way the noise was, if mine ear be true,*
> *My best guide now; me thought it was the sound*
> *Of Riot, and ill manag'd Merriment,*
> *Such as the jocond Flute, or gamesom Pipe*
> *Stirs up among the loose unletter'd Hinds,*
> *When for their teeming Flocks, and granges full*
> *In wanton dance they praise the bounteous Pan,*
> *And thank the gods amiss. I should be loath*
> *To meet the rudenesse and swill'd insolence*
> *Of such late Wassailers; yet O where els*
> *Shall I inform my unacquainted feet?*

Besides, I am all smugged up, all adorned for the party, all ready for the rout.

Yet, how hot it will be in there, up that flight of stairs to where they wassail in swilled insolence! How loudly shall I have to shout, to hear myself above all the ill-managed merriment! None will hear what I shout: I shall hear what no other shouts; all will be jocund revelry, with perhaps now and then an olive, a cheese straw, a glass of sherry or tomato juice, or a little sausage on a little stick. That is all very well when one is in the mood, and an excellent manner of employing an evening. But am I not also very well where I am, sitting in my car?

> *Hence vain deluding joyes,*
> *The brood of folly without father bred,*
> *How little you bested,*
> *Or fill the fixed mind with all your toyes!*

I turn my back on you; I trundle down small dim streets to the embankment, and along the dark, lit river, the night air, so delightful, so unwholesome, fanning my face and blowing through my hair, the wedge of a yellow moon, like a slice of cheese, rippling in black water among a myriad city lights. Tomato juice, strong drink, sausages, friendly faces, shouting wassailing and wit, I have rejected for lethargy, solitude, encharioted ease. I glide furtively home through streets and parks and embed in my own easy chair, as if I had never planned another evening.

But I shall never know what I have missed. What enchanting encounters, what faces new or long unseen, or all too often met; what jests, quips, cranks, quiddities, tales! They are occurring even now, in those high, lit rooms from which I turned. I am very well where I am; I prefer to be where I am; but who was it who said, "God himself cannot give us back a lost party?"

PARTIES

PARTIES

LET me die (as Melantha would say), but this will be a good party. See how many people are flocking in at the door, gay butterflies, bright birds all silkily emplumed, or glossily black and white, with tails like tails of ravens hanging down behind. How fast they flock,

> *As thick and numberless*
> *As the gay motes that people the sun beams!*

What a noise already they make! Already they are gay, benign, inebriate, they drink and eat like to a harpy—Oh, Lord, walk this way—I see a couple, I'll give you their history. In that corner, close to the hock cup, poets stand grouped; tolerable poets, better poets, definitely poor poets, poeticules, poetitos, poetasters. (Poets have coined more derogatory names for other poets than any other professional men have done, is it not so? That is because they feel very strongly about poetry and about other poets.) They speak of poetry as they drink hock cup and eat olives. Spender, Barker, Day Lewis, Auden, Pudney, Isherwood, they mention these, they argue about the latest works of each; poetomachia rages. Near them is a Roman Catholic group; these do not go in for poetry but wit; they drink deep and sing gay songs. Then there are novelists; I always think novelists rather noisy, do not you? Let us move out of earshot. There stand three publishers, telling jovial stories of the frolic Greeks. Or is it about some books they hope to publish? I cannot catch the words; all speak, none hearkens. On the sofa near me two women murmur mysteriously one to another; one looks informed, and as if she knew the secrets of every one in the room; she seems the wisest aunt telling the saddest tale. I am not near enough to hear it.

What will happen at this party? Anything may happen. A man has just come in who stands charmingly on his head at parties. Perhaps he will stand on his head to-night. I hope that he will stand on his head. That is what people should do at parties of pleasure; it gives parties of pleasure the right note. At least, so I think, though to Cleisthenes the despot of Sikyon it seemed in the highest degree unseemly that his daughter's suitor should dance on a table on his head at a banquet. This only shows how times have changed since the days of Cleisthenes; if I had a daughter, I would present her immediately to a suitor who did that, and gladly would she go to him.

Other parties of pleasure which have been held come into my mind. Agathon's party, into which Aristodemus gate-crashed, on the specious suggestion of Socrates that "to the feasts of the good the good unbidden go," and at which they praised love and Alcibiades complained of Socrates. That was a good party; I have heard that there are such parties now, but they do not come my way. Then I think of Trimalchio's party, where they began with dormice rolled in honey and poppy-seed, sausages, damsons, pomegranate seeds, and peahens' eggs containing each a fat becafico in spiced yolk of egg, and went on with a great dish of the signs of the Zodiac, and then really began to eat, every now and then washing their hands in wine. That was a vulgar party, a gluttonous, ill-bred Roman party; I should not like to be at that party. I would rather be at an English rout, assembly, or conversazione, nibbling dainty rout-cakes and sipping spiced wine, while the card tables are set out and the tea is brought in. Or at a party at the Royal Society's, where experiments in gravity and levity occur, bowls of goldfish are weighed before and after the goldfish are removed from them, fruits are frozen stiff, Æolian harps make music, and pyrophones their fiery moan. This is not a party such as that. Still, anything, or nearly anything, might happen at it.

There is a levity, a light and glittering quality, among the guests, as of revel routs on tiptoe for a feast. We quaff champagne, we gulp ices, we sit down with pencils and paper, we shall write a poem line by line. Some people leave the room, to return and perform for us; it is all most diverting. We eat again, we drink again; some are drunk, some sober. We all speak very loudly, but the time is past when I can hear much of what we say. It does not matter. It is a good party. Let me die but it is a good party.

So the brief night goes in babble and revel and wine.

It is bed-time, but we are still here. To go home would be so odd. They would say that one was not enjoying the party, to be leaving it so soon. One must stay, though the black bat night has flown, though no silence falls with the waking bird, no hush with the setting moon.

It is a good party, an admirable party: but can it be that parties of pleasure go on just the fraction of a second too long?

PLAY-GOING

PLAY-GOING

I AM, on the whole, entertained by these agreeable cheats. At their best, they divert and please beyond measure; at their worst (which often occurs), they embarrass and fatigue. But to sit and watch the curtain rise on the mummers who will strut and mime for us for two hours of an evening to make us sport is an excitement never stale. They will perhaps display to us some lively tragedy: caught in a very torrent, tempest and whirlwind of passion, they will saw the air with their hands and tear a passion to tatters, to very rags. Hamlet would have had them whipped for this; but for my part, I like to see them at it; I consider that this is partly what they are put on that raised daïs to do. They are in a fiction, in a dream of passion, and so, indeed, am I. Like Sir Thomas Browne, "I can weep most seriously at a play, and receive with true passion the counterfeit grief of those known and professed impostures." 'Tis true, they do often imitate humanity most abominably; but humanity we can see anywhere; it imitates itself; I would scarce cross the street to watch it. Yet here, set on this platform strutting above a row of lights, I will watch it for two hours (not, I think, for longer). On a stage meal I hang entranced, though I would not lift my eyes from my newspaper to see the same meal off-stage. I will delight in a stage dog, a stage baby, a stage quarrel, though all three are ever with us in the world without, and I think nothing of any of them. I will think with admiration, how well he said that! how wittily she took it! when I hear words well and wittily spoken all about me, and scarcely pause to mark them.

But sometimes the words are good words, well and wittily, or gravely and beautifully, written, and then how my pleasure is doubled; no, trebled, for there is the pleasure of the words, the pleasure of the speaking, and the pleasure of the fitness of the two conjoined. Should I ever hear, as I never yet have heard, the right Oberon sitting on a promontory to hear a mermaid on a dolphin's back, the right Titania deploring the confusing of the seasons, the right Prospero rounding our little life with a sleep, the right Macbeth in the tomorrow and to-morrow lines, the right Cleopatra in "The crown o' the earth doth melt. . . . And there is nothing left remarkable beneath the visiting moon," and in the asp speech (which I have heard said to break the heart, but not on the stage), the right Beatrice, Rosalind, and Millamant in look, voice, and wit all joined, the right Restoration sparks to body forth the Restoration comic spirit . . . but so one might go on for ever: should I ever hear these (as I have, once or twice, heard the right Hamlet), to be at the play would be to peer at heaven; such pleasure is more than one dare hope to purchase for the price of a plush seat. Normally, one must be content, or malcontent, with lovely lines blurred or flattened or coarsened in the speaking, or with plain speeches well enough spoken, as they are, or so it sounds to me, in most modern plays that I see.

Well enough, anyhow, for a theatre full of people to sit absorbed, smiling, laughing, moved, throughout the spectacle they have bought. We are, I suppose, easily entertained, and it was never hard to split the ears of the groundlings; even Punch and Judy will do that in the streets. As I said, there is that in the raised platform, the set piece, the ordination of players, the purchase of seats, which confers on common speeches and actions some strange cachet of prestige.

Anyhow, for my part I am pleased with these guileless impostures, and would watch them more often had I but more time, did the seats cost less, and would the play but run straight on without those dreary intervals that now break its thread and waste our time. If playacting should ever cease among the human race, which, after so many thousand years of mumming, would seem improbable, it will be the intervals which will kill it. There is not enough time in a crowded human life to waste hours of it doing nothing in a theatre, removed from all other occupations, and unprovided with the spectacle we gave up an evening to see. Music should fill these spaces, or a puppet show, or what not, if the play must pause.

PRETTY CREATURES

PRETTY CREATURES

THEY strut and trip around us, all shapes, all sizes, all colours, all species (for even a pretty little black curly-tailed pig is at times to be admired, and the infant rhinoceros has indubitable charms). We may enquire, with Montaigne, what this beauty is that so pleases, and whether it has existence outside the individual eye and taste; we know that it has not, and that this in no degree diminishes its power to ravish and entice. "The preeminence in beauty, which Plato ascribeth unto the spherical figure, the Epicureans refer the same unto the pyramidal or squat." . . . All the better, since Plato and the Epicureans are thereby both pleased. I dote on that gazelle, that tall, light-stepping girl with her slant eyes, her smooth and high-held head, her broad and smiling mouth; you on that fluffy kitten, that small and dainty person, with eyes large and round, clustering curls, pink roses in her cheeks. As to that, I dote on her also, as on all pretty creatures, from the sailing golden eagle to the gilded fly, from the splendid muscled athlete to the chubby babe in bath.

We are excelled, as we know, by many living creatures, earthly, airy, and marine. Yet this awkward and lumbering human biped has also power to ravish, and that not only its fellow-humans, who may be prejudiced in its favour, but those very creatures who, we think, so manifestly excel it. Fishes, notoriously amorous of the human race, have leaped from the water to the land if their angler be fair of face, have crowded round lovely bathers in embarrassing shoals, have carried beautiful boys across oceans. Unicorns have always loved young virgins to the point of rashness; lions, tigers and wolves have followed beautiful youths and maidens with no anthropophagous dreams, merely to dote on their faces and forms; birds have lost their heads altogether—

When he was by, the birds such pleasure took
That some would sing, some others in their bills
Would bring him mulberries, and ripe red cherries,
He fed them with his sight, they him with berries.

While, as to dragons, they have frequently doted to distraction, forgetting their own kind in their attachment to some handsome human creature.

If our dumb friends, then, can so admire our curious form, perhaps ejaculating when they see it the thanksgiving of the Hebrew, "Blessed be the Lord, who has made his creatures in such strange diversity of shapes," how much more should we. And do. For, if there is one thing for which we have ever admired one another, it is for our beauty. Whatever strange chance arrangement of features and colour it may be that pleases any given race, tribe, period, or personal taste, however little it may please any other race, tribe, or person, still, there it is, triumphantly, absurdly, irrationally victorious, enchanting such beholders as are to it susceptible. Beauty, as the intoxicated but truthful Comus remarked, is nature's brag. This amazing, confounding, admirable, amiable Beauty, than which in all Nature's treasure there is nothing so majestical and sacred, nothing so divine, lovely, precious, 'tis nature's crown, gold and glory—see where it goes, tripping and pacing about the common streets, about shop floors, uttering through its curled vermilion lips genteel remarks concerning art silk camiknickers and hose, swaggering in old flannels about ancient college courts, singing, bronzed and limber, behind mules on Apennine paths, running and tumbling with hoop and ball in Kensington Gardens, speaking rich Californian to us in darkened palaces, lounging about raised platforms above footlights. Beauty can do with us what it wills; more effectual on a jury, as Phryne showed, is a prisoner's handsome appearance than any eloquence of counsel: not only was Phryne, "following" (as reporters would say) the exhibition of her person to the court, discharged without a stain on her character (or without further stains than it had previously borne), but "those intemperate young men of Greece" erected to her eternal memory, with infinite cost, a golden image.

And here our best Athenians seem owls indeed (as someone remarks somewhere about something else): for who would desire a golden image of a beautiful lady? I should not look twice at Phryne in that hard and yellow metal. The very charm of beauty is its moving evanescence, its fleeting hue and swift-sliding shape, that turns this way and that like a leaf on the wind, like the running sea in shadow and sun. Beauty vanishes, beauty passes: living beauty fixed in metal, all chained up in alabaster, is a poor and chilly thing.

Lounge, trip, stride and run around me, then, oh lovely creatures of all sizes, ages, hues and shapes. You are a garden of bright flowers, a forest of saplings, like the young sapling shoot on Delos of which Nausicaa minded Odysseus; you are a very bestiary of such lithe and bright-eyed creatures as one may encounter leaping and slinking about jungle paths, or about ferny parks at Whipsnade, or prisoned in the small bright capitals of monkish missals. Speak not, oh beauteous idiots; move all in muted beauty like the moon; delight my eyes, and assault not my ears with your harsh or pretty jungle cries. I have no illusions about you; I know your limitations, and all I beg of you is that you will remain within them, and so continue to please.

READING

READING

HERE is one of the oddest of the odd inventions which man has sought out, this conveying to one another by marks scratched on paper thoughts privately conceived in the mind. It shows, as all the arts show, the infinite publicism of humankind, the sociability, the interdependence, which cannot endure to have a thought, to conceive a tale, a tune, a picture, an arrangement of words, or anything else, but all must forthwith be informed of it. And how avidly we run to be informed; we have already consumed many thousands of tales, poems, essays, and what not, but we are never satiate, we are greedy always for more. We begin the day by running our eyes over those multi-paged printed rags which furnish us with potted selections of events which have occurred during the last twenty-four hours. What excitement! Here are countries plunging into war, politicians making speeches, governments, aeroplanes and motor-cars crashing right and left, murders, thefts and revolutions, Britons flung into foreign goals, Etonians bowled by other Etonians in 1887 (they have remembered it ever since, amid all the uproar and confusion of life), outbreaks of healthy-Aryan-national-sentiment in Germany, of sacred egoism in Italy, of foot-and-mouth disease in Berkshire.

It has all occurred many times before, it will all occur many times again, but still I devour the pages with eager appetite, stimulated and mildly stunned. My newspaper makes me realise, in the improbable event of my ever forgetting it, on to what an exciting, what a tumultuous world, the sun and I matutinally rise.

Having risen, I endeavour for a time to bound my reading by what I regard as my proper studies, that is, by the requirements of such labours as I am at the moment committed to. These requirements, generously interpreted, may take me almost anywhere. They may take me, for example, to my dictionary; and, having heaved one of the somewhat ponderous volumes of this mighty work from its shelf (this is one of the main ways in which I keep in good athletic training) I continue to read in it at random, since it would be waste to heave it back at once. I need not expatiate on the inexhaustible pleasure to be extracted from the perusal of this dictionary, from the tasting of this various feast of language, etymology, and elegant extracts from all the periods of English literature. In this enticing pastime a whole morning may fleet itself idly away.

Or, on some slight pretext, the other works that beckon from my shelves like sirens from enchanted seas may win me to them, and, soon oblivious of the reason for my plunge, I am swimming in those deep voluminous seas, among poetry, masques, plays, history, lives, diaries, letters, zoology, navigations and explorations. These, last, above the rest, have the siren's power to drug and to detain. For they are, I suppose, what the

psychologists call, in their uncouth tongue, wish-fulfil-
ment, or dream-sublimation. They take you travelling
over the globe, and with no further trouble than the
lazy flick of a page. Why, as Samuel Purchas introduc-
ing his collection of travellers' tales, so plausibly asked,
travel, when you can get all the benefits of doing so
and suffer none of its damages, by reading of the
travels of others? Why should gentlemen adventure
themselves to see the fashions of other countries, where
their souls and bodies find temptations to a twofold
whoredom, and bring home a few smattering terms,
flattering garbs, apish cringes, foppish fancies, foolish
guises and disguises, the vanities of neighbour nations
(I name not Naples) without furthering their knowledge of God, the world or themselves? For his part,
for the benefit both of those who cannot travel far and
those who cannot travel virtuously, he offers "a world
of travellers to their domestic entertainment."

In brief, he recommends to us his travelogue, in
which "both elephants may swim in deep voluminous
seas, and such as want either lust or leisure may single
out what author or voyage shall best fit to his profit or
his pleasure." He would have us arm-chair travellers,
and well he knew how to play on our indolence.

Here, then, we sit, as he suggests, at home and in
peace under the shadow of our own vine and fig, and
from the shore behold with safety and delight the dangerous navigations and expeditions of explorers, view-
ing their war-like fights in the watery plain as from
a fortified tower, enjoying the sweet contemplation

of their laborious actions. Most commodiously we peregrinate with Marco Polo over Persia, Thibet, Turkestan, and to the court of Khublai Khan; with Spanish Conquistadores and English pirate merchants to Mexico, the Indies, and the New World; with Portugal friars about Abyssinia; with the Hollanders to the Java seas; with King Solomon's navy to Ophir; with Captain William Hawkins, hindered all the way by proud injurious Portugals and wily Jesuits, to the court of the Great Mogul; with Sir John Hawkins in the *Jesus* to take five hundred negroes on the New Guinea coast and make vent of them to Spaniards in the Indies; with the good ship *Dog* to the Mexique Bay; with Captain Knox to the wild Highlands of Ceylon; with Thomas Gage, the disgruntled Jesuit, over Guatemala; with John Chilton over all New Spain, among Indians who dared not eat him for fear he might have the pox; with Anthony Knivet plundering chests of silver from the cells of Portugal friars in Brazil, eating the bark of cinnamon-trees at Port Famine, encountering cannibals, a crocodile, and a great dead whale lying on the shore like a ship grown with moss. We may visit the island of Ferro and see that tree which rains continually; or chase after those flitting isles near Teneriffe which, when men approach them, they vanish; or behold the islands off Scotland swimming after the manner of the ancient Cyclades and flitting up and down in the water, the sport of tempests; on these same islands you may see (and still without moving a step nearer the Scotch express) trees from whose fruit falling into running water ducks and geese do grow. "Whoever took possession of the huge oceans, made procession round about the vast earth? Whoever discovered new constellations, saluted the frozen poles, subjected the burning zones?" Whoever may have done so, I am as good as they, and far more at ease, sitting in my arm-chair and following them about the world with my eyes, doped and lulled with their enchanting lies. Without putting out a hand but to turn a page, I break off a sugar cane and suck it, drop into my mouth pears dripping honey, pluck store of oysters from the boughs of trees (but these have a flash taste), gather barnacle geese from the barnacle-trees, smell the sweetness of great lemon woods, watch Sierra Leonians slithering up high palm-trees to fill gourds with palmito wine, eat wood fruits called beninganions and beguills, as big as apples and tasting like strawberries, taste cooked friar, but reject it as unwholesome, visit the Castle at Agra, where in a fair court every noon the Rajah sees elephants, lions and buffles fight, and so on to Lahore, the way set on both sides with mulberry-trees; watch a Christian ape at the court of King Jahanjar pick out the name of Christ from those of twelve prophets shuffled in a bag, tearing up the eleven others with distaste; sail up the river Quame for gold, elephants' teeth, ambergris and slaves; find turtles' eggs with Roger Barlow in the Indies, unicorns' horns with Sir John Hawkins in Florida; watch from the Florida beach the sea-fowl chase the flying fish; sail among these huge icy mountains which make such a dashing and crashing one against another in green Arctic seas; voyage, in brief, all oceans, peregrinate all lands, taste all foods, meet all people, enjoy all pleasures.

Meet all people. Yes; my humble dwelling-room becomes a salon, where I receive, without even troubling to rise or bow, an extraordinary miscellaneous crowd or rabble of persons, chattering in all tongues on all topics, in verse, in stately prose, in strolling, colloquial late-Stuart slang, in round and booming Johnsonian, in demure and ladylike Austenian, in sly and delicate Proustian, in gay modern English and French. Many are pompous, foolish, absurd, many have wit, many have ideas, many have neither. Some are wicked above the ordinary, some of a virtue only found among the angels and among earthly citizens of bygone centuries; of these my flat is not worthy, they shine oddly in it. Among them move people "so beastly that they put themself to no manner of labour, but study only how to take their neighbours for to eat them." Theological controversialists too I entertain; I hear the schoolmen thunder against one another on subtle points of doctrine, Jesuits and Jansenists furiously raging together, Puritan and Anglican at it hammer and tongs, non-Jurors smitten by the See of Bangor, the higher mathematics by that of Cloyne. Yet I do not greatly encourage these religious thunderings; I welcome more often blander and gayer guests, finding them apter for a salon. I prefer the urbane smile, the elegant jest, the fit phrase, the lovely line, the strange adventure, the subtle thought, or the sounding period of the historian.

At times, too, I like my salon to become a zoo, a bestiary, a setting for the infinitely strange habits of animals, of unicorns, elephants, dragons, manticoras, remoras, sea-serpents, dolphins, turtles, sparrow-camels, panthers, cockatrices, chameleons, and others of their curious kind.

Another and still more indolent salon I hold in my bed at night, in the hour before sleep. The guests here are of a different kind, less disturbing and exciting, for it does not do to be disturbed and excited before sleep. Poetry will not do at this hour, nor prose of a past and more splendid age. It is an hour reserved for the narrative fiction or biography of the present moment. As I drift in this agreeable ship towards sleep, I marvel drowsily at its good craftsmanship. How charmingly A writes, I think; how ingenious is B, how C's quick wit makes me smile, how D holds the attention nailed fast, so that if one slips a word one loses a sense. How sharp an irony sparkles from E's pages, how amiable a jester is F, how sound a workman G. How well they, for the most part, write. (Those who do not, do not detain me for more than a few pages.) Surely, I sleepily reflect, the standard of writing has climbed up and up through the past two decades. When I was young, we did not, I am sure, write as well as we nearly all write now. The standard has risen. There are, I believe, floods of tosh; fortunately, unless one is a publisher or a reviewer, one need not see it. But there is enough that interests, pleases or entertains to fill the ante-somnial hour night by night with company good enough for the occasion, which is all that one should demand of current literature.

So much for the home salon. One attends, also, the salons of others. There are within my reach two great places of entertainment. One is in a pleasant square; here one roams at will about gridded galleries, reading what one chooses, removing books by armfuls and leaving them scattered on tables to find their own ways back, or taking them away, either after being entered in ledgers if one is a person of probity, or concealed in despatch-cases if one is a thief; for this library is a notable hunting-ground for thieves; frail human nature has signally failed under the strain of seeing so many books at once, and the biblioklept, one of the lowest of God's creatures, may be prowling next you along those quiet corridors, his stealthy hand plucking the desired fruit from the bough and stowing it furtively away.

This is less possible in the other great London resort of readers, where they know better than to trust us. Here we are fed liberally, afforded every kindness, but we are marked men and women, we cannot easily steal away with pockets full of volumes. Unless, indeed, we chanced to be newcomers, gave false names, and were careful not to return. Something in this sort might, I suppose, be managed. But for most of us the strait and narrow way of rectitude is indicated.

We can, however, lick our fingers to turn the pages. I have been told that some readers even lick the pages direct with the tongue, but this habit is, I believe, confined to those who have been allowed special access to books not generally accessible, and denotes some peculiar pleasure.

For my part, I find it enough to sit drowsily in a great circular room, my wants supplied (in God's good time) by attendant elves, a great bank climbing volume by volume about me, shutting me off from the inky little student writing a research thesis on my right, and from the patriarch from the far deserts of Arabia on my left, leaving me dreamily alone, transcribing from crabbed texts in a crabbed hand, languishing agreeably in that hot-house clime, all the books in the world (or as near as makes no matter to me) within the call of a written order.

What is the extraordinary pleasure that we derive from this pastime? Why do we forget everything for it, feel by it transported, enlarged, enslaved, freed, impassioned, enlivened, soothed, drugged, delighted, distressed, entertained, sharpened in wits, ennobled in soul, winged in imagination, gratified in humour, stirred to pity, rage, love, rapture, enthusiasm, creation, zeal for learning, infinite zest and curiosity for life? I do not know, nor anyone.

And, in the end, it wears down our eyes, never intended for this strange and crabbed use, so that we have to read through discs of magnifying glass. As to our health—"the man whom about midnight, when others take their rest, thou seest come out of his study meagre-looking . . . squalid, and spauling, dost thou think that plodding on his books he doth seek how he shall become an honester man. . . . ? There is no such matter."

No, indeed. Still, he has enjoyed his reading.

SHOPPING ABROAD

SHOPPING ABROAD

How strange it is, this passion that assaults the breast
when the foot treads foreign earth; this lust to acquire,
to carry away, to convey home in suitcases wretched
pelting trifles which in our native land we should be
the first (or so we hope) to disdain! With how fond
pleasure have I purchased bronze models (green with
antichità) of the Temple of Vesta in the shape of an
inkpot, and of the extant fragments of the various
structures that were reared, regardless of expense, to
honour the triumphing monarchs and gods of Imperial
Rome. With what delight have I bought in Taormina
tiny painted mule-carts; in Palermo sections of a
similar but larger cart, that would be of use, so one
hoped, for a bed-head, for a wardrobe door, for a
screen; in Naples coral charms against the evil eye and
mother-of-pearl spoons; in Pisa the leaning tower in
marble; in Athens the Erictheum in alabaster; (the
seventh Lord Elgin, stirred by this passion on a grander
scale, bore away, as we know, the Parthenon frieze); in
Mexico painted pots, and walnut shells containing, preserved behind glass, tiny Mexicans; in New Mexico
rugs and silver brooches made by Hopës; in Monterey
huge abalone shells; in Florida twigs of worthless
branch coral; in Spain fans illustrated with bull-fights;

in Canada moccasins with fringes, and little canoes with Indians; in Quimper crockery; and I have known those who did worse than this in Brittany, and returned laden with giant oak dressers, cupboards and beds.

What is this foolish, this unconsidered mercery, this itch for having, this covetous desire for alien trifles, that mads the brain in foreign climes, emptying purse and bursting suitcases? What is it but that xenophilous lust that sent our great pirate traders a-merchandising to far coasts, plundering them for goods at which they would not have looked had they lain at their doors? Once across the seas, the bartering instinct wakes; we march into shops and markets, inquiring the prices of objects whose sole claim on our desire is their transmarinity; being informed, we exclaim "Troppo, troppo," "Trop cher," "Demasiado," or "Zu viel"; we make as if to walk out, but we are detained, met half way, the seller climbs down, we up, the bargain is clinched; we emerge happy, clasping in covetous hands this new and charming fragment of Abroad, which is to beautify, cheer and decorate our island life.

So Raleigh doubtless felt, a-homing from Guiana and Virginia with gold dust, tobacco, and potatoes in his hands; so Captain Smith, returning from Turkey with coffee beans; so Drake, sailing away from San Domingo, his fleet cargoes with the loot of that sacked city; so Warren Hastings retiring from Oude laden with the pearls of its Begums; so all British travellers preparing to re-cross to their island with pockets full of the bric-à-brac of foreign parts.

They will lie about our homes, bright and brittle intimations of past joy. This little coconut: when I caress its withered head, all the palm-fringed silver sands of the Florida Keys shimmer again before me. This gay and tiny cart, collecting dust on the chimneypiece, carries me along the hot white road from Palermo to Monreale. These walnut-dwelling Mexicans, with their bundles and their tall straw hats, take me to a lemon-grown plaza, warm and wan in pale dust beneath an orange moon, where mandolins eternally play and tiny *burros* trot patiently, bearing Mexican gentlemen larger than themselves. In this abalone shell sings the Pacific surf, beating on Fishermen's Pier and against the piles of Pop Ernest's Restaurant, where Spanish sailors lounge. To caress this bronze gondola is to see green water lapping against the rust-red brick walls of Renaissance palaces, to hear staccato cries, "Sta-i," "Premé!" while to touch this Vestal ink-pot is to stir all the dust of Imperial Rome.

The snag? Yes, you have guessed it, you who have also shopped abroad. Suitcases filled already to repletion, how should they distend themselves to absorb these alien objects? They will not; it cannot be done. More suitcases must be purchased; cheap, exotic suitcases; more, and more, and more. . . .

SHOWING OFF

SHOWING OFF

WHAT is that you say you have done? Walked across
Jamaica on your hands? That is nothing at all. Besides,
it is probably not true. I once rode a dolphin across the
Messina straits. And swam from Corsica to Sardinia. I
ate seventy plums at one go, stones and all. I lived
six days in a tree. I won a prize on the ocean for chalk-
ing a pig's head. I won a prize at school for the quarter
mile. And for the high jump. I wrote out "The Ride
from Ghent to Aix" backwards. What did you say?
You have a certificate of *what?* Signed by the Pope. . . .
And three children. . . . Well, that was just a mistake,
wasn't it; you should have told him. . . . You gave ring-
worm to two archbishops? I really do not see that that
is much to boast of. You converted Cherokee Indians
when you were six? That is better. And had a tract
written about you, called "How little —— came to
Jesus." That is better still. But I have had my conversion prayed for by a Lama. No, not in Thibet; we met
in Syracuse. Yes, I know Sicily well. I understand
Sicilian more or less. And modern Greek. Yes, I know
Greece. I didn't go there with one of those mass
cruises; I went separately: I always think one sees it
better that way. I know Greek literature pretty thoroughly. And Greek history, of course. I have done
some verse translations of the Anthology that they tell

me are not so bad. So bad as what? As most people's, of course. However that may be, I felt thoroughly at home in Greece. How long was I there? Well, I don't quite remember; certainly over a week. I had to get on to Constantinople after that. And then to Russia. I saw something of Stalin in Moscow; he wanted me to write something about my impressions, but the fact was I hadn't any, because I knew no Russian to speak of. You need to know a language really colloquially before you can begin to understand the people, I always say. The way I know Catalan, Mallorquin, and even Basque. Oh, yes, I know quite a lot of Basque words.

Well, where was I? Yes, after Moscow I visited Germany. I saw Goering and Goebbels; the Führer would not see me; he had heard I was coming, and ordered Goering and Goebbels to send for me for an interview; they tried to trap me in conversation into saying something they could have arrested me for, but I wouldn't. Though I let them see my views all right. How they loathed me! They knew I was a writer of more influence in England than . . . well, than most writers, I suppose I might say . . . anyhow, they were scared to death. However, there was nothing they could get me on. I got safely over into France, and had a gay week in Paris; I know so many people there, I'm never at a loss. I had another proposal, too. Then I visited the place in Normandy my ancestors came from in 1066; they tell me one of the angels in the roof has my face, and that it must have been done from one of our family, in the thirteenth century. I must say, I always *feel*

Norman, a kind of arrogant feeling, as if the English were under my heel. Not that ancestors matter: one makes one's own way. What do you say? Your ancestors were Saxon thegns? Well, some of mine were British druids. I always feel at home at Stonehenge. And I learnt to talk Welsh and Breton as easily as possible. And, of course, I could learn Erse and Gaelic too, if I cared to. But they don't seem very much use today, do they?

Well, I must go; I am going on to Buckingham Palace. No, quite a small party, I believe; no, the Garden Party is quite another thing; everyone is asked there. This one is for Ruth Draper; she is going to give a command performance, to a few special people. I don't know why *I* should be asked . . . oh, you are going, too? How strange. . . .

Well, now they know what I am; now they, left behind in the house, are talking of me, saying it is not often one meets anyone at once so intelligent, cultured, travelled, handsome, modest, witty and gay. I strut down the street, I get into my car, start the engine, trundle along Piccadilly. How well I drive! Traffic to right of me, traffic to left of me, volleys and thunders; I wriggle unscathed through the middle of it. I am thinking still of the lunch party I have left. I am trying to make sense of something someone seemed to be murmuring to someone else as the door shut behind me.

What was she saying? It sounded like "Ho, ho! I am the Toad. . . ." But that does not seem to make sense, so it must have been something else. . . .

SOLITUDE

SOLITUDE

WHAT is this sensuous pleasure, this tide of starry peace, that flows around me like a Milky Way, making a heavenly music in mine ears? What is this space, this liberty, this balmy ease, that floods about me like a blue and buoyant sea, at once sustaining, stimulating and soothing? How rich, how sharply hued, how pregnant with meaning, does the universe appear, where but an hour since it was a wild and wandering globe lost in chaos and the chattering of voices. I am alone. I can look, listen, feel, apprehend, without muffling presences to bound imagination's flight, to maintain those human contacts which remind us always that we are gregarious creatures, running together in flocks. Good company is delightful bondage; to be alone is to be free. I may do what I choose, within the limits of capacity and means. So long as I keep myself unspotted from the world, there is none to stay or molest me or prevent me in my doings. I can, if I will, stand on my head, and none to comment, question, smile, or stare. The mountain nymph, sweet Liberty, trips hand in hand with me to the court of the reeling goddess with the zoneless waist and wandering eyes, there to tread that lordly pleasure house that none can share. Drony solitude; Dr. Johnson's ill-meant adjective hums lovely in my ears, bringing to them the idle boom of bees among honeyed blooms, the sweetness of that happy garden state while Man there walked without a mate.

> *But 'twas beyond a Mortal's share*
> *To wander solitary there . . .*

and has, alas, been increasedly beyond a mortal's share ever since, what with teeming humanity and minishing gardens. Nevertheless, the two Paradises in one are still at times accessible. Aloneness can still be attained, by those who have the will to it. A perpetual and enforced state, it might cloy and irk; an occasional adventure, it might be wasted, unpractised, difficult; a frequent yet not immoderate indulgence, its drony beauty binds and snares, enspells and yet sets free; we come to it as prisoners for a space enlarged, as thirsty men to a tavern.

> *If thou canst get but thither,*
> *There grows the flower of Peace,*
> *The Rose that cannot wither,*
> *Thy fortress, and thy ease.*

Attired with stars we sit, or we can fly, or we can run, and joy shall overtake us as a flood.

But Dr. Johnson said one day, "Solitude is dangerous to reason, without being favourable to virtue. Remember" (continued he) "that the solitary mortal is certainly luxurious, probably superstitious, and possibly mad."

Well, there is no state without its drawbacks.

SUNDAY

SUNDAY

ALL Sundays are not blue and hot and gay. In these
latitudes few Sundays are blue and hot, though there
is about Sunday a leisured gaiety that sets it, even when
it is grey and cold, to what Milton called a dominical
jig. Sunday strolls, sings, peals bells, dances, eats,
drinks, sleeps, talks, in a care-free, slippered ease; it is
different from Monday and the rest; it smiles like a
holiday, it simpers like the spring; it is, as George
Herbert observed, a day of mirth. Dr. Johnson held
that there should be relaxation, but no levity, that one
may walk, but not throw stones at birds. In fact, there
is both relaxation and levity; there is also love, for the
parks, lanes, street corners, cinemas and country places
are thick enturbed with turtling couples who make the
Cupid. Religion, too, much obtains; in churches there
is singing, chanting, preaching, praying, and celebration of mysteries, in all the tongues in the world alive
and dead, besides great ringing of bells. There is a
hum of life, of pleasure, of leisure, of piety, of tranquillity.

For my part, when I say "Sunday," I see a span of
hours both blue and hot, a vault of sky without clouds,
a floor of sea without waves and of white sand without shade. All Sundays, even in that place, were not

blue and hot, but that is how I see them. No lessons; a day of pleasure, of bathing, wading, canoeing, reading, writing, taking out the goat, racing the rabbits, climbing trees and rocks, hearing the chanting of processions winding by. Gay stalls in the town, bells clanging, nets coming in, rounders on the shore in the evening, sitting in the ivy on the top of the *orto* wall. Time for everything; no lessons: that was, and always is, the point, the thing that sets Sunday apart. Even a grey Sunday, a wet Sunday, a cold English winter Sunday, when we can but stay indoors and read and eat and talk, is still a day of pleasure, since from our journal labours we do rest.

And yet, what assaults, what besiegements of misplaced pious intention, has the day of the sun, probably at all periods, endured! It would seem that there cannot be a day of pleasure and repose set up by man but some other men must seek to entrammel it in tedious bonds. We say, on one day in seven it is good to rest and make holiday and make our congee to the gods, laying aside diurnal toils. We say, put the spade and axe away, for we will do no work to-day. Then arise law-givers, priests, prophets, leaders, police, who enforce this gay intention, hedge it about with rigorous rule. Rightly, no doubt, since the heart of man is covetous and cruel, and there will beyond doubt enter into it the project of causing slaves and menials to perform those profitable labours for him from which himself he rests. Thus does his own native wickedness create tedious rules and fetters for sinful man. Then, since the lust to make rules, to embond and enshackle others, grows apace in the hearts of law-givers, they took this cheerful day, this septimanal jewel in the week's belt of toil, and set it about with prickles and with bars, minded to keep not only toil but mirth at bay. To this unavailing task Christendom early applied itself. Constantine forbade pleasurable spectacles in the circus, and all public celebrations and sports, except only that of the torture and execution of criminals. Charlemagne, that tremendous Sabbatarian, followed by emperors, kings, popes, and priests, sternly continued the losing battle against Sunday pleasures. The history of Sunday in all lands is the history of Pleasure, that indomitable goddess, assaulted, bound and fettered, even down to this day, but valorously slipping now a shackle, now an imprisoning bar, negligently ignoring bondage, and dancing and playing on the green, denounced by church and state, thundered at by minions of the law, kept at bay by parents (who shut up little Samuel Johnson and made him read the *Whole Duty of Man* of a Sunday), menaced by papal decretals, by Genevan gowns, by Town Councils, by every tyrant in office, and yet breaking free, and yet enlarged, and yet on dominical pleasure bent, so that Sunday has ever been a glad day despite them all.

For by th'Almighty this great Holy-day
Was not ordain'd to dance, to mask and play,
To slug in sloth, and languish in delights. . . .

Thus preceptors of all creeds and all lands have spoken down the ages. And Humanity has answered, not with defiance, but with that serene, intractable negligence that in the end defeats all law. Saying little about it, the majority have slugged in sloth and languished in delights each Sunday, thus recompensing themselves for the hard tedium of the week's travail.

And here it comes again, the sun's day, the Lord's day, merry and free and holy and bland. Hey! what comes here along, with bell-chiming and ringing? 'Tis Sunday a-coming. . . . Hey! there again, how the bells they shake it! Come, come, ladies, come ladies out. . . .

Yes, that is all very well: but how am I to walk out, when my shoes that I forgot to fetch yesterday are still at the cobbler's, and the cobbler has shut his shop? And how shall I be happy staying in, when the book I meant to read is still in the library, and the library presents a shuttered face? Further, my wireless accumulator has run out, and I shall not hear Kreisler to-night, for those who keep accumulators have shut them behind locked doors and gone holidaying. I am frustrate, cribbed and baulked, to make an English holiday.

TAKING UMBRAGE

TAKING UMBRAGE

VERY good, then, very well; by all means attend to everyone else in the shop before me, though I was waiting here before any of them. There is such a thing as fair turns, as serving people in the order in which they come, but you do not seem to bother about that here. That old lady, that young man, both were after me, but you go up to each in turn, you say, "What may I do for you?" and they, being deficient in sense of honour and fair play, both hasten to tell you, instead of saying, "It is not yet my turn. You must serve that woman over there first." Very good; I will make no movement to call attention to myself; I will stand here waiting, while you attend to these interlopers, and then to others who have pushed in even since they did. I suppose that in time someone will think of inquiring of me my pleasure, instead of hastening by with half questioning glances which I refuse to meet. I will not, even by a look, convey that I demand to be served; I coldly stand and wait: I have taken umbrage. I am wrapped in silence, an umbrageous mantle; I am shadowed about and umbraged with my pride; I have taken pet. I have joined the great company of the umbraged of all time. How they hover and shadow umbrageously around! Monarchs and subjects, priests, physicians, lovers, authors, actors, heroes, prophets and gods, all cloaked in dudgeon, uttering high, cold words of proud offence, or else, wordless, wreaking deeds of vengeful ire. Kings, queens, emperors, outraged beyond mercy, exclaiming, "Who will rid me of this traitor?" "Little man, little man. . . ." "Fling him to the fishes!" Offended gods and goddesses jealous of their honour and their rights; Apollo flaying upstart rival musical performers, Achelous the river god transforming into islands the naiads who omitted him from a party, Latona and her archer twins potting at the insolently excessive progeny of Niobe, Diana enstagging Actæon for this ill-judged bagniospection, Zeus and Hera each so unflaggingly alert for slights, so ingeniously efficient in avenging them, Jehovah, so easily provoked to wrath, so apt to turn his face from his Israelites, so quick to send them plagues. The umbrage of deities has been, very naturally, fruitful and well gratified, above that of others. But by no means contemptible has been that of authors, of actors, of prima donnas, and leading men; of John Milton, Alexander Pope, Lady Mary Montague, Dean Swift, Lord Byron, Samuel Coleridge, Andrew Marvell, Ben Jonson, and, for that matter, practically all who have lived by the pen. With what gusto have these beaten their pens into swords, envenomed them, and plunged them into the quivering breasts of rivals, calumniators, mockers, and reviewers. How their turbulent and impassioned phrases beat about me, darkening the air like eagles' wings! Could I but utter some of them, how those who pass me by in neglect would start and pale and fly to do my bidding. Then there are too the huge grievances of parents, more particularly against daughters; the Capulets, Lear, Egeus, Squire Western, and the rest, all loud with vexation, disappointment and threats. "Full of vexation come I, with complaints" . . . that has been the burden of parental life down the ages. A thousand umbrages wing and buzz about me like exultant wasps. Doctors, hearing that rivals have been called in, and refusing in their turn to come when implored. "Certainly not: I hear that you have Dr. Blank now. . . ." Slighted lovers, slighting back, avenging neglect with cold pride. And, hovering and looming, a huge and purple cloud, the tremendous umbrage of Churchmen down the ages. A thunderous cloud, out of which come forth mighty claps and darting fires that play about the heads of heretics and disputants, striking upstart dogmatists to annihilation, sending empassioned eristics and direful fulminations over sea and land. The terrific voices of offended clergymen quiver and vibrate in the air about me. How they would strike these oblivious so-called salesmen to nothingness, could the salesmen but hear what I hear!

So, compassed about with so great a cloud of witnesses, luxuriantly umbraged, I stand and wait for the moment when one of these minions will turn to me at last with "What may I do for you?" I shall not immediately tell them what they may do for me; I shall tell them first what they have already done to me; how they have kept me waiting long past my turn, kept me for ten full minutes out of my busy life; how this is the last visit I shall pay them; how, the next time that I require a new fountain pen, I shall seek it elsewhere; how no flourishing commerce can be built up on a foundation of injustice, on a system of breaking the law of Fair Turns; how I did, indeed, half an hour ago, wish to purchase a pen, but, during the hour that has elapsed since then, I have lost the desire, I no longer require a pen, or anything but a couch on which to repose after my two hours' waiting; how, when my friends ask me where they shall buy pens, I shall reply, "Anywhere but at Messrs. Penley & Inkman's, for there they do not attend to you, but keep you waiting from three to six, and then they shut and you have to go away unserved"; how . . .

"What can I show you, madam?"

"Oh, is it you at last? Fountain pens, please. I have been waiting . . ."

"Certainly, madam. What make of pen do you require?"

They will never know, it seems, of my umbrage.

TALKING ABOUT A NEW CAR

TALKING ABOUT A NEW CAR

YES, the time has come. The two low gears make a noise like the large cats at the Zoo at lunch-time, and even top is like the large cats purring *after* lunch, or like an aeroplane zooming just overhead. I must have a car which makes noises like small cats purring in their sleep, or, at worst, like an aeroplane a thousand feet up. Besides, the thing takes so long to pick up speed. And it groans. And drinks petrol like a fish. And it can't get up Primrose Hill on second now. And . . . but what I mean to say is, it's eight years old, and has had its day, and I am looking about for another. Still, did you say? Yes, I always look about for another.

Do you like the Garnet ten-four? The Grasshopper, you know. It is roomy, accelerates from standing like an arrow from the bow, and climbs like a cat. Only sixty; but one seldom really wants to do more than that, I find. And thirty-five to the gallon, they say; I dare say actually thirty. The only question is, how well it holds the road. I must say, I incline to the Grasshopper. A green one, should you say? Or a red? Or beige? Of course black or navy is less *noticeable*. What I mean is, supposing a policeman saw a lot of cars all speeding, he might pick out the brightest coloured for an example. And a bright colour shows up more in the night, if it is left in the street without lights, or over time in a park. Black or navy melts into the night. But then beige melts into the day better, I suppose. And green into the parks, supposing one were doing rather over twenty there. Not red, I think; that does not seem to melt into anything. Into an accident, you say? Pray do not let us talk like that; I do not have accidents.

See, here is a Rapide 1933—cost £350, and offered for eighty. Yet it is exactly like new, the advertisement says. Super-clean, absolutely indistinguishable from new. Mileage nominal. Then why, I wonder. . . . Oh, I see, it says why—owner giving up driving. I suppose he has had his licence suspended. Perhaps he is in prison. I wonder what the accident was, and how much the Rapide was damaged. They put them together again so strangely sometimes. Some friends of mine bought a car which had been in collision, and its back axle had been put in again upside down. I might go and look at the Rapide's inside. Outside, it sounds charming—splendid condition, red leather upholstery, long wheel base, everything de luxe, silent engine, super appearance. What a delightful car. One wonders why the owner so seldom used it, in two years—why, I mean, he only did a nominal number of miles. No, he does not say how many; the number is nominal, like other numbers, but he seems to have forgotten its name.

Then here is a Daimler which cost approximately

£1,285 in 1932. Approximately. One would think one would remember spending such a sum as that. I suppose he put it out of his mind at once, not caring to dwell on it, and now has mislaid both the bill and his pass-book. Perhaps actually it did not cost quite so much. Anyhow it is in super condition, like the Rapide, and he will take £275, though there is absolutely no depreciation. A fluid fly-wheel, too; and fitted with smart owner-driver . . . dear me, how odd. Well, anyhow one cannot buy a Daimler, of course, though one likes to toy with the idea.

Let us turn to the Austins and Morrises. The year really does not seem to matter, since they are all indistinguishable from brand new in every way. I wonder how many miles and years it does take to make a car distinguishable from brand new. How different they are from people! Here is an Austin Seven De Luxe Sun Saloon, 1931, for £10. Now I call that cheap. Oh, I see, it says "down." There would be a little more payment to follow. . . . Well, never mind, I do not want an Austin Seven, it is quite too small. What about the 1933 Morris Ten? I always say, you know where you are with a Morris. But wait, here is a Moonbeam 1928, deposit £3. Luxury riding, for small outlay. Looks like 1933. . . .

Well, really, it is all almost too confusing. Do you think perhaps I had better go on with the old car for the present? After all, when I have bought a new one, I shall not be able to talk about all the others so well, shall I? As it is, I seem to possess them all, which is delightful.

The only drawback is that I get given so many cards with the names of car salesmen on them, and these gentlemen are all so kind in taking me out for runs and writing to me that I hate the thought of disappointing any of them. Yet on the whole I think I had better disappoint them all, and go on as I am. After all, you know where you are with your old car.

TELLING TRAVELLERS' TALES

TELLING TRAVELLERS' TALES

YES, I had a marvellous time. I went first to . . . But I will get my picture postcards; I can explain it all better with them. No, indeed, no bother at all; no, really, I should like to—that is, if you would care to see them—or even if you would not. See, here they are. Yes, they *are* a great many; yes, everywhere I went I got some; they make a complete picture diary of the trip. Look, this is the Acropolis . . . but that is too soon, they are in the wrong order; Marseille comes first; see, here is Marseille; I have six of Marseille. That one is the Rue Cannebière; and there we have the Château d'If. That is the old port, and . . . dear me, this is Progreso, Yucatan, and must have got into the wrong set, for that was quite another trip. Yes, I must show you my Mexican postcards too; no, really, no trouble at all, I like it; but we'll do the Greek trip first. There is Marseille harbour, which we saw, of course, as we steamed away. Our next stop was Genoa; that one is the west porch of the Duomo; here is a close-up of one of the lions. This is the south aisle, and . . . Oh, must you really? I'm so sorry. It is quite early still, and we've only got to Genoa. There is all Greece to come; we had the most marvellous adventures there. I must tell you all about it next time. Well, if you really must go. . . . It has been delightful to see you. I like to tell you about

Abroad, for I know you understand. I remember all
those postcards you showed me of Malta last year . . .
or was it Portugal? . . . Yes; well, now it's my turn, is
it not?

My turn. Yes, and I intend to take it. I hold them
with my skinny hand, "There was a ship," quoth I.
The dinner guests they beat their breasts, yet cannot
choose but hear. They listen like a three years' child;
the mariner has his will. And that is really all the
mariner can expect, in view of the strong travel-tale-
resistance that flourishes in most modern human beings.
It occurs to few travellers, as it occurred to Æneas, to
be actually requested to describe their trip. Dido, with
charming feminine and queenly courtesy, said to her
just-arrived guest after supper, "Now relate to us your
wanderings from their first beginnings"; whereupon
they all settled down to it, every tongue was still, every
ear attentive, and Æneas, reposing upon his couch, began the tale of his long ramble, enabled by his hostess's
courtesy to preface it by saying that it was the last
subject he desired to dwell on, it being so sad and
himself so sleepy, but that, since she longed to hear of
it, he would oblige her. He was allowed to proceed
uninterrupted with a travelogue which must have taken
quite three hours. Odysseus took similar advantage of
the kindly invitation of King Alcinous, on his visit to
Scheria. Few of us meet with such good fortune; in
fact, but for our picture postcards, we should find
ourselves hard put to it to get any way at all without
interruption, without the travels of other people break-

ing roughly in. The Wedding Guest was, one imagines, very young, and had not yet travelled himself, or one cannot but think that he would have put up a more efficient travel-tale-resistance than he did. Most returned travellers seek in vain their Desdemona, who shall seriously incline to hear of antres vast and deserts idle, and of the cannibals that each other eat, the Anthropophagi, and men whose heads do grow beneath their shoulders. These last peculiar people have usually had but a poor reception; practically all travellers have told of them, but the diffidence with which both the ancients, and such bold enlarging Elizabethans as Sir Walter Raleigh, put them forward (he wished he had brought one home with him, to put the matter out of doubt) seems to indicate that those reporting them were, except by the credulent Desdemona, found on the far side of the line which divides liars from mere bores. For one has to be on one's guard; one must not try one's audience too far. An air of elegant reticence is often advisable; a touch of Herodotean scepticism; and Raleigh's lofty, "And if to speak of them were not tedious and vulgar . . ." will sound the right note of sophisticated deprecation of our own adventures, and is a good preliminary to speaking of them just the same.

But it seems to have been always recognised that relating one's rambles viva voce is a somewhat chancy business; the wisest aunt telling the saddest tale is not always listened to; hence travellers have usually committed their trips to paper, knowing that the printed word breaks resistance down where the human voice does but strengthen it. Thus, it has always been the custom for returned travellers to write travel books, whether in the form of fictional narrative, or of true; and it is said that this form of literature is the greatest in bulk of any in the world. So, if you can prevail on none to give ear to your saga, or eye to your post-cards and your photographs, take a pen and write your heart out, as did the lusty voyagers of all time. Join that great romantic company of enlarging travellers who have held it more commendable to publish unto the world what they have seen and done abroad than to permit it to fester perilously in their bosoms. Tell the world how the ice-bergs crashed around your bark, how fishes flew for you and whales spouted, how you spied a ruined city in a jungle and a phœnix in a date-tree, a gila monster up a barrel cactus, a chaparral cock fighting a rattlesnake in the mesquite, a golden eagle carrying a lamb, anthropophagi making a meal of a missionary; a unicorn with his head on a virgin's knee; and any other of the strange relations of authors that you think good. Do not fear to expand: you are in admirable company; the best company, many hold, in the world. It is a fine bold thing you have done, this going abroad, and you deserve that people shall hear about it. Telling them, you will relive your happy journeyings. . . . Ah, me, how Delos, dropped from heaven, swung moorless on a violet sea. . . .

Let me show you my postcards; indeed no, it is no trouble at all. . . .

TURTLES IN HYDE PARK

TURTLES IN HYDE PARK

THEY lie close-locked, arms entwined, face on face, oblivious, loving, and dumb, strewn like chrysalises about the littered, burnt-up August sward. No speech passes; they bill, but do not coo; it is better so. John Donne has described their state.

> *And whilst our souls negotiate there,*
> *We like sepulchral statues lay:*
> *All day the same our postures were,*
> *And we said nothing, all the day.*

Another poet, a century later, mentions a young woman less wise than these:

> *Sabina has a thousand charms*
> *To captivate my heart;*
> *Her lovely eyes are Cupid's arms,*
> *And every look a dart:*
> *But when the beauteous idiot speaks,*
> *She cures me of my pain;*
> *Her tongue the servile fetters breaks*
> *And frees her slave again.*
>
> *Had Nature to Sabina lent*
> *Beauty with reason crowned. . . .*

But Nature is seldom thus lavish, and Sabina and her swain are happier dumb. So dumb they lie, turtling it in the turtle-haunted parks, thick as autumnal leaves that strow the brooks in Vallombrosa, while the night dews gather on the grass, and the Park exhales the warm stale breath of the long summer's day, and policemen, simply and plainly clad, pace among their flock, their firm expressions saying, "Thus far and no farther," and the keepers blow their whistles for time up. To bed, to bed, kind turtles now!

Delightful it is to see Cupid thus busy, to see lovers thus emparadised in this park of pleasure. But how we stumble over them as we walk! Impossible to help it, since there are so many billing pairs, so little space between each pair and the next. Not all our stumbling can break that subliminal peace in which they lie intranced; but, through the pillowing clouds of love on which they rest, does some faint jar from the lower world ever so faintly shake them, as one passer-by after another trips over them, kicking their entwined forms? Love gives courage; loves gives oblivion; they do not appear to notice. It is we who trip and fall.

Yes, sweet turtles, to bed! It is really time you removed yourselves out of our way.

WALKING

WALKING

WHAT is there in this so primitive, so outmoded motion of legs and body that gives so fine a lusty pleasure to some of those who practise it? One leg before the other, feet planted swiftly on the ground in turn, lifted, planted again, carrying the whole person, slowly, indeed, (as traffic travels to-day) but surely, (until intelligence revolts and the motion ceases) along: wherein lies the charm of this animal pastime? I suppose in the fact that we are, in fact, animals, and the mere exercise of the body pleases. "The race of wild pedestrian animals," says Timæus, "came from those who had no philosophy in any of their thoughts, and never considered at all about the nature of the heavens, because they had ceased to use the courses of the head, and followed the guidance of those parts of the soul which surround the breast." Very true; and so we stride along, walking vegetables, one with the earth we traverse, empty of thought, lazily gluttonous of eye and ear and nose, scrambling up hill, pushing through holt and hanger, emerging on to thorn-grown, wind-swept, close-cropped down, below which spreads a far, hazy glitter of sea, plunging down the hill's steep shoulder into green bottoms where cressy brooks wind, following ancient footpaths where they run on ancient maps, paths sometimes long lost and forgotten, leading over broken stiles and blocked hedge-gaps, across foot-bridges long vanished, over fields long ploughed, through copses and thickets which have run riot and made impenetrable with their jungly growth what was once the way through the woods. The path broadens; it becomes for a space a deep dark lane, alder- and hazel-hidden, sunk in mud. It is called on the map, for half a mile, Cockshut Lane. It comes to Standfast Barn, plunges through a gap into Cuckoo Copse, becomes again a footpath, tilts up across two steep fields towards the beech-hangered ridge of Farewell Hill. And so on and along, and it will lead you round by the Oakhangers to Cheese-combe Farm, and home by the moors.

What is there to it? You walk, you look, you hear, you smell; life arranges itself easily into a sen-suous dream, a feast of sound, sight, scent, and al-ways that light, swinging motion carrying you along, without effort, without thought. So doubtless, do the other animals feel, padding the earth, with their soft, quick feet, nose to ground, ears pricked, eyes bright. Yet they have an effect of following something; they seem ever on the chase, questing and nosing after some dream they have. Here I have the advantage of them; I follow nothing, beyond sometimes a path. I walk for walking's sake; do they also engage in this pastime, that some consider so odd? In America, I am told, it is not practised; if you walk, it is because you have no means to drive or ride.

Some walkers, such as Socrates, seem to walk only

to talk, or to think about something, and even so they prefer to stroll about cities. Socrates enjoyed the green bank of Ilissus when he was taken there, since it offered a charming spot wherein to rest and bathe his feet while he was read to; but (said Phædrus to him), when you are in the country you are like a stranger being led about by a guide. I think you never venture even outside the gates. Very true, my good friend (said Socrates), and I hope you will excuse me when you hear the reason, which is that I am a lover of knowledge, and the men who dwell in the city are my teachers, and not the trees or the country. But (added he), you have found a spell with which to draw me into the country, as hungry cows are led by waving before them a bough or a fruit. For only hold up in like manner a book before me, and you may lead me all round Attica and over the wide world. And now, having arrived, I intend to lie down, and do you choose any posture in which you can read best. Begin.

A hopeless walker, you see; the kind of walker who would read a book as he walked, or argue about the absolute, or want to sit down and rest after a hundred yards; a walker only suited to pacing meditatively about cloister or peristyle, or strolling about the agora, hailing friends and hearing news. Walking for pleasure should not be an intelligent, discursive, gossiping or bookish pastime; it should be solitary and dumb, placid and vacant of mind, an unimpeded, undistracted error over earth's face, leg after leg, corporeal frame and urgent soul to timeless motion set.

So on we go and on, in delicious rhythm, until we tire. And the worst of that is that, when we tire, we are so many miles from home, and have to walk as many again to reach it, so that by the time we arrive there, we are fatigued indeed. A little forethought, you say, will prevent this? Very true; but walkers are not intelligent, and do not think ahead; they walk themselves weary, and develop all manner of ailments in the process. A good walk, you say, is worth them all? Again, very true.

WRITING

WRITING

OF ALL the animals, man appears to be the only one who enjoys this peculiar pleasure of writing. This is unfortunate, as it would be interesting to read the written works of the dog, the cat, the fox, the hog, the hippopotamus, and others, did they commit any. Besides, it would keep them quiet. Or would it not? Now that I come to think of it, I do not know that the human beings who write most are the quietest. Still, for the time being, the occupation of writing does prevent those engaged on it from making much noise, beyond that emitted by the typewriter or the pen. Parents find this, and all intelligent parents instruct their children early in the part, provide them with pencils and paper, and leave them to it. I myself was early thus instructed and, though I am told that for some time my only form of literary activity was to write in block capitals on every available space the boast "I CAN WRITE," still, this I assiduously did. Step by step, graduated to higher forms of the art; very early I collaborated in the fictional efforts of my elder sister, and a little later commenced poet. By the age of seven, I was a confirmed addict. Ever since, the pile of my written works has grown and grown;

it has always been to me, if a rather shame-making, yet an insidious amusement.

Wherein lies its charm? Mainly, I believe, in arranging words in patterns, as if they were bricks, or flowers, or lumps of paint. That is, to me. Heaven never, I think, destined me for a story-teller, and stories are the form of literary activity which give me the least pleasure. I am one of the world's least efficient novelists; I cannot invent good stories, or care what becomes of the people of whom I write. I have heard novelists complain that their characters run away with their books and do what they like with them. This must be somewhat disconcerting, like driving an omnibus whose steering-wheel, accelerator and brake are liable to be seized by the passengers. My passengers know their places, and that they are there to afford me the art and pleasure of driving. Are there not, for that matter, already enough people in the world, without these beings intruded from my imagination? Shall they puff themselves up because they are allowed on paper? I have heard of novelists who say that, while they are creating a novel, the people in it are ever with them, accompanying them on walks, for all I know on drives (though this must be distracting in traffic) to the bath, to bed itself. This must be a terrible experience; rather than allow the people in my novels to worry me like that, I should give up writing novels altogether. No; my people are retiring, elusive, and apt not to come even when I require them. I do not blame them. They no doubt wish that they were the slaves of a more ardent novelist, who would permit them to live with her. To be regarded as of less importance than the etymology and development of the meanest word in the dictionary, must be galling.

And so we come to words, those precious gems of queer shapes and gay colours, sharp angles and soft contours, shades of meaning laid one over the other down history, so that for those far back one must delve among the lost and lovely litter that strews the centuries. Such delving has rewards as rich, as stirring to the word-haunted fancy, as the delving into the deeps of human motive and emotion has to the novelist of psychology, or the weaving of intricate plot and counterplot to the story-teller, or the laying down of subtle clues to the detective problemist. Words, living and ghostly, the quick and the dead, crowd and jostle the otherwise too empty corridors of my mind, to the exclusion, doubtless, of much else that should be there. How charmingly they flit before me, heavy laden with their honey like bees, yet light on the wing; slipping shadowy out from dusty corners, hiding once more, eluding my reach, pirouetting in the air above me, now too light, too quick, to be caught in my net, now floating down, like feathers, like snowflakes, to my hands. They arrange themselves in the most elegant odd patterns; they sound the strangest sweet euphonious notes; they flute and sing and taber, and disappear, like apparitions, with a curious perfume and a most melodious twang. Or they abide my question; they offer their pedigrees for my inspection; I trace back their ancestry, noting their diverse uses, modes, offspring, kin, transformations, transplantations, somersaults, spellings, dignities, degradations, lines and phrases which have enambered them for ever, phrases and lines which they have themselves immortally enkindled. To move among this bright, strange, often fabulous herd of beings, to summon them at my will, to fasten them on to paper like flies, that they may decorate it, this is the pleasure of writing. England, the pirate, has ransacked the countries of Europe for her speech: Greece, Rome, France, Germany, Scandinavia, have poured in tribute to her treasury, which shines and jingles with the most confused rich coinage in the world. To play with these mixed coins, to arrange them in juxtaposition, to entertain oneself with curious tropes, with meiosis, litotes, hyperbole, pleonasms, pedanticisms, to measure the words fitly to the thought, to be by turns bombastic, magniloquent, terse, flamboyant, minishing, to use Latinisms, Gallicisms, Hellenisms, Saxonisms, every ism in turn, to scatter our native riches like a spendthrift tossing gold—this is the pleasure of writing. It is this, rather than concern with relating of human beings, which can hold me thralled through a night, until, in the long street outside my high windows, the pale morning creeps, and the scavengers arrive with little carts to remove the last day's dust. It is dalliance with this pleasure that I promise myself when I think of work;

it is, alas, dalliance with it that too often abets me in my day-long and easily accomplished business of keeping work at arm's length. For to hunt language, to swim lazily in those enchanted seas, peering at "whatsoever time, or the heedless hand of blind chance, hath drawn from of old to this present in her huge drag-net, whether fish or seaweed, shells or shrubs, unpicked, unchosen," may well fill a day with such pleasure that to put pen to paper in the way of business, of getting on with some task in hand, seems too rude an interruption. Rather let me set down lines of verse, phrases of prose, experiments in rhythm and sound, images and pleasing devices, as they come into my mind, without relation to any larger work to be accomplished. Let me be an amateur of verse and prose, dealing in fragments only.

But here is a trouble and a hindrance, that has ever impeded and hampered the dilettante in his enjoyments: one believes that one has to live, and to live one must try to earn. And who will buy these fragments, unstrung, unset, without context or co-ordinated form? Who will buy the fish or seaweed, shells or shrubs, caught in my drag-net, scattered loosely like the twigs of white coral and the oyster shells with which Italian fisher lads pursue the foreigner, crying *Frutto del mare?* No one (heaven forgive readers and heaven help writers) desires such loose jetsam. They desire books. And, oh, God of literature and of achieved tasks, how incompetent do I feel adequately to produce these!

ABOUT THE AUTHOR

DAME ROSE MACAULAY (1881–1958) was born in Rugby and educated at Oxford High School and Cambridge College, Oxford. Born into an intellectually distinguished family (the eminent historian Thomas Babington Macaulay was a relative), Macaulay published her first book, *Abbots Verney*, in 1906. She wrote over fifty fiction and non-fiction titles including *The Pleasure of Ruins* and *The Towers of Trebizond*. She was appointed Dame Commander of the British Empire in 1958.